aubkay 2002@yahoo.com

Borrowed Time
On the Road to Nepal

Kay Donaldson

ISBN 978-0-9835557-0-4

Designed by Jodi Junkin

Photos by Kay Donaldson

PRINTED IN THE UNITED STATES OF AMERICA

For Baylie and Gage

May you never lose your love for reading,
or your desire to jump on your trampoline
with your crazy Grandma. I love you more
than you will ever fathom… until the day
you have grandchildren of your own,
and then you will suddenly understand.

Foreword by Kay Donaldson

"You should write a book." Heard it once, heard it a hundred times. Not sure why, but when my fingers start typing, the words flow out of my brain and onto the screen. I always felt I had it within me to write a book, but never knew what to write about. In the back of my mind, I always thought if I took a week away from my life, went to the Outer Banks of the Carolinas and sat on an isolated stretch of sandy beach somewhere, the inspiration would come. Then about the time I turned 50 and entered the healthcare arena after a 15-year stint working in the automotive engineering world, a healthcare HR-manager life sage, Bob Pruitt, reassured me that I didn't need to *go anywhere* to write a book. He told me, *"You already have everything that you need locked up inside of your brain; you just need to start writing."* Two years later, and two nights into a trip to Nepal, in the wee morning hours in the Norbu Linka Hotel in Kathmandu, I had a revelation that Bob Pruitt was right. God had brought me all the way around the globe to Nepal for a reason, and in the stillness of that night, I knew then and there that writing a book was to snap yet another piece of my life's puzzle into place. So here it is – my gift to Bob Pruitt, my family, and every other person in my life who has told me that I should write a book. The inspiration didn't come while sitting on a sandy beach, it came while spending 23 days in a journey to Nepal and India, where I experienced bamboo house building and had gray mud stuck under my fingernails, trekked through the Himalayans, visited the Taj Mahal, saw a tigress in the wild, and got sunburned while riding an elephant. And to think back and remember now that it all began with a benign question, hidden in the context of a simple email received from an emergency room nurse. "I'm coordinating an international Habitat for Humanity trip to build houses in Nepal, would you be interested in being on our team?"

Chapter 1

Friday, January 14, 2011

What an adventure! It started with a late August 2010 email from Marilyn Emmert, Parkview LaGrange Hospital (PLH) Emergency Room nurse by trade, international Habitat for Humanity coordinator by heart. Marilyn informed me that she was planning a trip to Nepal in January/February, 2011, and mentioned that she had an opening on her team if I was interested. She didn't want an answer right away; in fact she instead told me to go home and think about it over a weekend. I wrote her back on a Monday morning and told her I somehow felt I was being led to join her team (think that had anything to do with the fact that the thought of the trip had popped into my mind about 79 times that weekend?). I had come to know Marilyn when I worked as the executive assistant to the COO at PLH, which is a small 25-bed critical access hospital in LaGrange, Indiana. The hospital is centered in the middle of LaGrange County in northeast Indiana; a county with a high Amish population and matching high unemployment. Marilyn and her fellow ER co-workers always wore their heart on their sleeve, and each fall this compassionate ER team would donate its time coordinating an annual Amish children's safety fair at a local Amish school. That day was spent working with hundreds of elementary school children and their siblings and parents at educational booths and conducting hands-on learning experiments. They taught the benefits of healthy living and how to stay safe in the Amish community, where very young children are often expected to handle adult-type chores within their family structure. So there was that question, hidden amidst other details for the upcoming Amish Safety Fair: "I'm coordinating a Habitat for Humanity trip to build houses in Nepal, would you be interested in being on our team?" Marilyn also shared with me that Linda Patterson, another ER nurse was also on the trip team, along with Dr. John ("Doc") Egli and his wife, Deb. Doc is a local physician with privileges at the hospital, and he and Deb were experienced globe travelers. Everything that has happened during the past months has been a compilation of planning and preparation. First, I had to fill out a request for a three-week absence from my current executive assistant's job at our Parkview Health corporate office (approval was required, since I didn't have enough paid time off to cover the entire trip). Parkview Health is a 7-hospital, 7500-employee health system headquartered in Fort Wayne, Indiana, and I was very grateful when the paperwork came through, and I was granted permission for a leave from my job to make the trip. Over the next several weeks after I committed to being a part of Marilyn's Habitat team, the Eglis would be extremely helpful in guiding me through the process of obtaining an India visa (they had invited me to accompany them on a 3-day trip to India at the end of the Nepal adventure) and giving me some good insight on what to pack (or more importantly what to leave behind) for this trip. One of the last important boxes-to-check to solidify the trip, was my extraordinary mom, lovingly volunteering to ride herd at my house with my dogs (A.K.A. "the girls") while I was away. Flossie, a 17-lb. wire fox terrier, and Mabel, a 75-lb. miniature-black-angus-cow lab, absolutely loved "Grandma", and I knew they would soak up her 24/7 attention while I was gone. The mere thought of my 78-years-young petite mother, sleeping with that big honkin' black bag of concrete each night on the foot of my queen-sized bed, had me smiling. With the cost of my airline ticket and three-weeks of rooms and food in Nepal, I never would have been able to afford to kennel the girls and make the trip. My mom's loving offer to live with her furry grandchildren in my absence was the final catalyst for my definite "yes" back to Marilyn. The planning and preparation soon mirrored a line of neatly stacked falling dominoes: receiving countless email updates from Marilyn on what to expect on this adventure, passport/visa paperwork which at times seemed even more blinding than a game of pin-the-tail-on-the-donkey, updating my tetanus shot (which leaves your arm feeling like you've been sucker punched by Marlin Steury in third grade on the East Auburn Elementary playground when you had a crush on him), taking a regimen of pills for malaria and typhoid fever, registering with HFH for a global trip application and being approved as a part of Marilyn's HFH Global Village team for this journey, and making plans with Tina Colwell, our administrative manager at Parkview for coverage for my responsibilities while I was away (she is a true peach). Since a snowfall is practically inevitable in Indiana in the months of January and February, my adult son Alex agreed to watch for snow on my driveway and plow it with the snow blade on the front of his truck during my absence. My daughter Abby, and her boyfriend Jason, thoughtfully reassured me that they would check up on her grandma and dogs at my house (which I know left Jason internally relieved that Mabel wasn't going to be sleeping on their bed each night ☺). So on a bone-chilling Friday morning in January, I finished packing my Gander Mountain cargo bag, and threw another carry-on and my hiking daypack in my car. After hugging Mom and telling my dogs I would be back in three weeks, out the door I went. Even though I shed a few tears while pulling away, I somehow felt like a God wink was happening; like this trip was going to be an answer to something in my life, I just couldn't see it clear enough to know what He had in store for me. As I drove towards the Egli home in Topeka to meet Doc and Deb for the ride to Chicago O'Hare, I called three of my dear friends, Judi Hamilton, Pauline Smith, and Carol Musser, one more time to reassure them I was

7

going to be safe. Judi had been battling brain/lung cancer for the past 15 months, Pauline had recently endured some difficult physical trials in her own life, and when I ran into Carol right before Christmas, she told me she had recently been diagnosed with a serious liver condition. With that in the back of my brain, I just wanted to hear each of their voices one more time before leaving. I reached Judi, and then Pauline, one after the other and chatted to them, but ended up leaving a voice message on Carol's home phone when no one answered. I arrived at the Egli's home near Topeka around 10:30am. Theirs is a sprawling home built atop a knoll in the middle of countless country acres, with beautiful Amish woodwork and vaulted ceilings. The walls of their great room are adorned with mounted trophy heads that Doc had shot on hunting trips afar over the years; it's really a beautiful home. As if this wasn't his first winter rodeo, Doc had me park my car at a strategic angle in their driveway, knowing that if we got several inches of snow while we were gone, it would be easier to get a running start out of their drive and down the hill when we returned in three weeks (little did he know what was ahead of us). I left my Droid and car keys inside their house (I recall having to pry my Droid out of my hands which left me a little no-technology-for-three-weeks shaky), and we secured our luggage into the back of Deb's Tahoe. Doc had to check on a patient at PLH, and Deb had to print something at Doc's Topeka office. I hopped into Doc's truck to head to the hospital with him to see my past co-workers there, and everybody sure was shocked to see me show up at the hospital. I had fun hugging friends and past co-workers while Doc made his rounds, and then we left the hospital to meet up with Deb at her parent's house in Shipshewana. We drove to the South Bend airport with Deb's parents (who would then take Deb's Tahoe back to Shipshewana) to catch the shuttle to O'Hare, and thought for sure we wouldn't make it in time because we got out of Amish-Dodge later than they wanted to. Upon arriving at the airport, Doc took off to see if they still had seats available on the shuttle bus, and when we found out the bus was still loading, we quickly threw our luggage onboard, Deb and John said good-bye to her parents, and off we went. We got to Chicago in fine airport-limo-bus fashion, and then waited several hours until we could check our luggage. My mom had sent along two thick Amish-created rag rugs for the HFH families, and even though they were heavy, they were a great gift for her to share with our HFH team as a house-warming present once the homes were completed. Due to the Egli bags being heavier than anticipated when leaving home, we made some switches in our luggage as I had extra space after switching my rugs into my carry-on. We waited for the gate to open, and in the end we found out we could check two bags free of charge, so all of our packing and re-arranging didn't matter anyway. It quickly became very apparent that we were definitely in the minority in the check-in line. The three of us Midwestern Milquetoast folks from Amishville were quite amused and wished that we had a picture taken from overhead of the three of us gringos standing in line, amidst about 450+ Nepalese, Indians, and United Arabic Emirates/Abu Dhabi dark-hair-dark-skinned citizens, all heading back home. We decided to grab a quick bite before the plane took off, and to my disgust, I spent $12 on a simple airport veggie snack tray! As departure time drew near, our gate waiting area became packed, and Deb mentioned that she got a HUGE whiff of curry/Indian smell, and she said that scent made her nauseous. I told her that I didn't have any perfume with me in my carry-on, but that I could offer her some Crest toothpaste, which she could smear under her nose (we joked that instead of cocaine, she could snort a little Crest!). Since my Droid was now safely sitting in Deb's kitchen in Topeka, I borrowed Doc's phone and called my daughter Abby, to let her know that we had arrived in Chicago safely and were waiting to board. I quickly picked up on the fact that during these hours at this gate of the terminal, and possibly in this culture, kids pretty much did whatever they wanted to, without any parent control or intervention. While I was sitting there on thinly-padded gate chairs waiting for the Etihad Airlines 7:55pm departure, we saw countless examples of that… Indian/Nepalese children, standing in front of their parents, continually screaming and demanding things, droning/babbling on and on and on, while the parents seemed oblivious. Deb said that she had experienced that many times before, but I was amazed to watch it happen right in front of me. One of the families never made their children sit down to eat; instead they followed their little boy around with a spoon being fed from a bowl of what appeared to be yogurt, saying "eat, eat, eat, eat." We were finally allowed to board the loaded-to-capacity jet, and the flight attendants looked so sharp; they all had on dark jade green suits, with cream-colored silk scarves adorning the berets on their heads. During take-off, the display on the LED panels on the seats in front of us showed the take-off from a camera on the nose of the plane, so you felt like you were inside of a video game. I looked across the aisle, and Deb was pretending that she had her hands on the controls of the plane, so I yelled over, "Pull up! Pull up!" and she yelled back, "Not yet!" The flight lasted about 14 hours, of which I think I slept a mere hour. I was blessed to have the opportunity to be seated next to Mr.-Abu-Dhabi-A.D.D.- nervous-leg-twitch, with all of the symptoms of major Attention Deficit Disorder or fear of flying. His left leg (of course it had to be the leg that was on the side next to me!) never quit shaking the entire flight, and even when he looked like he was asleep, I couldn't help but notice that his leg would shake while he was snoring! It was an incredible experience to be locked in a jet with that many foreign people during such a long flight, with nowhere to escape when all of those sleepy children started crying. It was about out of control at times. There was a little child in the row behind me, and I think he screamed for 20 minutes non-stop at about 1:30 in the morning, to the point I felt somebody was going to get up and demand that they do something with him. In the parents' defense, where were they supposed to walk the child? Up and down the aisle throughout the entire plane and wake up all 400 trying-to-sleep passengers? I watched seven movies on this flight, practically back-to-back, because I could not convince myself to get comfortable enough to fall asleep next to Mr. Jerky. It was unnerving to think that a jumbo jet could fly for that many hours, without re-fueling, and still take off with that much fuel on board. Kind of scary to think about.

Chapter 2

Saturday, January 15, 2011

We finally arrived in Abu Dhabi 14 hours later, and walked into a beautiful area of the airport where the multi-colored ceiling was an incredible work of craftsmanship. Mosaic tile, pieced together in a dome-shaped ceiling, in beautiful ocean blue and green shades (I took pictures). I fell in love with a stuffed camel at a gift shop, "Humphrey", and made the decision that I was going to stop and buy him when we came back through there on our way home. He had a "squeeze here" sticker affixed to his hump, and when you squeezed him, he let out the cutest camel grunt/growl. It was hilarious. It was interesting watching a game which I believe they called field ball, a combination of our basketball and soccer, on the flat-screen TV that hung in the terminal. The players would run down the field dribbling a soccer-size soft ball, but then when they got down the field to what appeared to be a soccer-like net, there was a defender and they could throw the ball at the net. We grabbed a bite in a little coffee shop while waiting for the gate to open, and then enjoyed looking at Doc's pictures of a scuba diving adventure that he had saved to his Notebook (where haven't these people been??). When the gate opened, we were again struck by the glaring fact that "we are definitely in the minority here!" The 200 square foot area was filled with Nepalese men, the majority of which we later understood were flying home from working jobs somewhere else to provide income for their families. There were only four women on the entire plane, with about 150 men; we stuck out like a sore thumb. The ticket person called Deb and I up to the ticket counter and boarded us first before any of the men (Doc was clear in the back of the line). We took off, had a snack, and then I proceeded to watch "The Social Network" on the in-flight movie channel, wrote in my journal, did some Sudoku, and took a nap while we were winging our way towards Delhi, India.

We landed in Delhi, and had some confusion about getting into the area of the airport we needed to be to go from Abu Dhabi to India (were we to go through the continental flights gate, or international flights gate?). I noticed these huge 12-foot high gold-cast hand symbols hanging above the customs gates countertop, with the fingers bent into what I thought were sign-language letters, but which I later learned were Yoga symbols. Since we had mistakenly turned and gone into the international flight portion of the airport, we then had to go through customs TWICE (as if entering into India, and then departing from India, as we were once again leaving for Nepal on the next flight), and they were practically anything but helpful. This was the first time that I had to go through the pat-down draped security booth, and there were two security female agents in there that talked the entire time and just did their searching very nonchalantly (my pockets were stuffed with my passport, camera, pens, Kleenex, etc., and they never even asked me to empty my pockets). By the grace of God (because He was the only one that seemed to be helping us) we found our way to our gate to sit and wait on the flight to Kathmandu, and started searching for a bathroom where we could brush our teeth to get some fresh breath after the long all-night flight. From this point forward (and until we returned back to Chicago), we no longer allowed ourselves to drink tap water, hoping to avoid all possibilities of unpurified water and developing diarrhea. We finally found a vending machine with bottled water inside, but since this was prior to converting

14

United States Dollars (USD) into rupees, we instead purchased two Diet Cokes at a gift shop to brush our teeth with in the terminal bathroom. Now that was a new combination for me... Crest and Diet Coke. Wowie-zowie! Kind of had me shaking my head like Mabel does after getting a strong whiff of skunk! We found a place to park our carry-on belongings in some empty seats to wait on the next flight to Kathmandu, and I grabbed my backpack and reached inside to grab my journal to start writing. Suddenly, I had this sickening feeling when I realized that I had apparently left my nice, new journal in the seatback pocket of the previous jet in my hurry to get the customs form filled out for our arrival into India. I searched through my entire backpack, and just wanted to vomit, as I had covered the front page of that journal with email addresses and phone numbers of family members (because I would be void of all of the info I had stored on my Droid, *my true inner brain*, which I had left back in the States for safety). That paper journal, given to me by my dad and step-mom for my 52nd birthday last fall was going to be my B-i-b-l-e for the entire trip, and it was definitely no longer locatable within the contents of my backpack. As one of my life-mentors would say, *"Oh cuss."* I went to the gate counter and asked the ticket agent for assistance, and she said they would try to call that gate if the plane hadn't taken off again and have someone search in the seatback pocket in front of seat 12C. They never did find it prior to our plane taking off, so I guess I was just out one nice birthday trip journal. I was totally bummed about that, and they said to check their lost and found on our return trip to India. Right... Right....

Chapter 3

Sunday, January 16, 2011

Our jet took off for Kathmandu, Nepal, and I sat by myself in window seat 12A, with John and Deb sitting several rows behind me. Got a little misty-eyed, thinking about how I had just lost that journal with my one connection to my kids with their email addresses, phone numbers, and about how much I already missed my family and my dogs. After a small in-flight meal, I proceeded to fall asleep so soundly that I completely missed flying over the Himalayan mountains near Mt. Everest (in fact, I was sleeping so hard, that when we landed and hit the tarmac in Kathmandu, my head jerked and I woke myself up!). The Egli's got the biggest bang out of me missing the sight of Mt. Everest-size mountains, it was funny (I think that was the hardest I had slept the entire trip so far). So there we were in Kathmandu; Bob Seger, eat your heart out! When flights land at the Kathmandu airport, the passengers are shuffled into small buses, for what ends up being a short 300-yard bus ride to the terminal (it would have been quicker to just let us walk). The sign on the Kathmandu airport wall read, "Welcome to Nepal. Mount Everest, 8848m". We filled out Nepal visa forms at an airport counter (Nepal is a country where you don't have to fill out a visa form weeks in advance like you do for India). We handed them $25 for a tourist visa, and we were in the country. It was mass confusion retrieving our luggage, and it was interesting to see how many folks on this incoming flight had tied boxes together with heavy string, for shipping their clothes in lieu of luggage (possibly a lot of those transit workers who couldn't afford luggage?). We found Puskal Adhikari, our Raya Tours connection, outside of the airport holding a "Habitat for Humanity" sign to draw our attention to him. After adorning our necks with welcoming scarves (a tradition I would see MANY times in this country), he loaded our stuff into a van and we drove through the streets of Kathmandu, with me gawking out the window at EVERYTHING. We were definitely in a part of the world that I had never experienced before, and my eyes and senses could hardly take it all in. I was riding in the very back of the extended van, and when I looked forward at Puskal, who was sitting in the front left seat of the van, and whom therefore I assumed was driving, he kept turning around talking to us. It began to freak me out that his eyes were NEVER on the road as he was always turned around talking to us, and yet we were moving forward and weaving through traffic like a panicked mouse heading back to his hole! FINALLY, I realized that in Nepal, everyone drives on the left-hand side of the road while sitting in the front RIGHT SEAT of the vehicle you were in. So Puskal wasn't the driver, he was the passenger, and was doing the whole tour-guide shtick; I just couldn't see that the steering wheel was on the right side of the vehicle, with the driving responsibilities adequately being handled by our driver! There were bicycles, mopeds, cars, vans, all driving in nonstop chaos, poverty, trash, people wearing not enough clothing to keep warm, SKINNY stray dogs, cows and goats along the street, brick buildings that looked like they had been bombed in Pearl Harbor or decayed by years of pollution, horns honking, newly-butchered chickens sitting out in the dirty dusty air, goats for sale tied to the front of stores, chickens/roosters running around, dogs barking, tires screeching, bamboo scaffolding poorly erected to repair buildings, etc. At one point when I saw a cow standing right smack dab in the middle of six lanes of traffic I screamed, "There's a cow!" and I thought Doc was gonna crack up laughing. We arrived at our Kathmandu refuge, the

Hotel Norbu Linka, located in the Thamel district of Kathmandu (which I was led to believe was owned by Lhakpa T. Sherpa, who had summited Mt. Everest on May 24, 2007). We found the rest of our 11-member Habitat for Humanity team sitting around a big coffee table in the chilly hotel lobby, deeply ensconced in a passionate game of Bananagrams. It was so nice to meet everybody! Along with John and Deb Egli, I was soon to spend the next days of my life with Felix Lozano from Tijuana, Mexico, and a trio of lifelong friends… Phil Rooney from Fairfax, Virginia, and Bill Vigneault and Steve Longo from Laguna Beach, California. Then there was of course our fearless team leader, Marilyn Emmert, and one of her fellow ER nurses from PLH, Linda Patterson, and the other two Midwesterners in the bunch, Larry and Cheryl Winger, who live not far from Purdue University near West Lafayette, Indiana. What a cool group of people. Our flight was the last to arrive into Nepal, so everyone else had been checked in and were waiting for us to show up so we could all go grab some lunch together. We newbies to the group dropped our luggage in a secure area of the hotel, grabbed our day packs, and we all walked about two blocks to the Thamel House Restaurant to eat together in an open-air patio. The pagoda-styled restaurant was built over a hundred years ago for an affluent Newar family; the floors were finished with locally made brick tile, and they had preserved much of the wood-carved doors and walls. The "age" of the city of Kathmandu seemed ancient, and it was apparent that this part of the globe was settled eons before my beloved hometown in Indiana. I ordered my first Nepali meal – fried cashews and chicken mo-mo. It was a delightful taste of things I had never tried before, and I liked it! My first impression of Kathmandu was that the air felt warm, but I was quick to discover that the second the sun started disappearing late in the afternoon in the pollution-screened-daylight, the temperatures quickly dropped and you found yourself scurrying back to your hotel for another layer of warmth. Even though this was their cold, winter season, I was amazed that there wasn't any heat per se in the hotel. The front door of the hotel was ALWAYS open, and the marble floors of the lobby seemed to keep the entry area as cold as an icebox. After grabbing my Cabela's hiking coat (thank goodness for that layer of wind-sheer-resistance), we returned to the streets of Thamel and shopped for a while, then went back to the hotel and made plans to meet in the lobby for the evening's activities in a couple of hours. Yes! This gave us time for a quick, much-needed post-jet-lag nap! The other team members already had rooms since we were the last to arrive, so Deb and I hauled our bags up two flights of stairs to a two twin-bed room and Doc squeezed into a room with one of the other guys. On the ledge outside of our freezing cold and un-homey room was a delft blue/gray pigeon, nesting behind a window air conditioning unit, and we enjoyed listening to her gentle deep-throat coo's, which was somehow warm and soothing in this frigid late afternoon environment. After a quick COLD whore's bath (as the water in the shower seemed to rival the room temperature), Deb and I were both chilled to the bone so I got into my luggage and retrieved Mom's thick rag rugs that had flown over here in my cargo bag. We unrolled a rug onto each of our twin beds, covering the paper-thin hotel comforters for an added layer of Mom-American-warmth and climbed underneath and took a quick-but-hard nap before Doc knocked on our room door for dinner. I will always remember how good it felt to stretch out horizontally for that quick nap, no matter how hard the mattress was, no matter how cold we were, it was a real treat to be able to do that after having to stay vertical on that long flight over here from the States. Down in the lobby we met up with our HFH team, where we departed on a memorable walk to a local restaurant. I don't think I will ever forget that walk. The sights, sounds, smells, and atmosphere will all be forever etched in my brain. It was dark, and cold and wet as it had rained during the end of our afternoon shopping trip. There we were, 11 tourists in this seemingly-God-forsaken city, all together with Puskal in a group, walking in quick fashion through dark cobblestone streets or on uneven broken sidewalks, with traffic flying by us. Our only sight-by-night vision was by car light or an occasional lamp glow from a local business prior to the daily lights going out in the city. There was a hum of generators kicking on and horns honking, amidst local aromas of fires, incense, sewage, etc. We arrived at the restaurant, and had such a wonderful evening experiencing their local Nepalese cuisine, traditional dancing, etc. All 11 of us welcomed-with-a-red-dot-on-the-forehead-foreigners sat cross-legged on the floor, atop thick red floor mats around a brown tablecloth-covered long table in a room with mustard-colored walls with many other low tables. We started off the meal with rice wine poured down from a gold vessel which the waitress held about three feet above the table. The wine burned the whole way down my throat, and to me it was like drinking lighter fluid (good thing there were Cokes and Everest beers available on the side). I found myself taking pictures of everything before I ate it, either because of the presentation or because of the kind of food they told me it was. At one point in the evening many of us got up and danced with the local entertainers, who were dressed in bright shiny dance costumes. It was one of those moments in my life where time stood still, and I let my brain capture and soak in the sights and sounds of everything around me, the music, us dancing up and down, holding hands in a circle, laughing, etc. There was even someone inside a stuffed peacock costume moving through all of the dinner tables! The peacock would lean over and pluck dollar bills out of your offered hands as it walked through the dining area. It was funny, and everyone was wondering how to create one of those costumes for use back in the States! We had such a great time telling stories and getting to know one another better over dinner. I was blessed to enjoy the opportunity to sit at the end of the table with Steve, (who at 70, was the gray-haired, tall, thin, hazel-eyed, tanned-face, California-ocean-beach-living, Mensa-card-carrying, Nook-Bananagrams-wizard, still-jogging-countless-times-a-week

21

kind of guy), Bill (nearing 70, dark-haired, suave-Maria-looking, Department of Commerce world-traveled, stand-up-shtick-comedy guy) and Phil (at age 72, red-headed, ruddy cheeked, warm-eyed brilliant-Navy-pilot guy who now volunteered as the treasurer at his church because of his razor-sharp accounting skills). Throughout the course of the evening, I began to hear parts of their half-a-century friendship story. Their memories serve them well, and Phil and Steve met each other in 1959 when they were midshipmen at the Naval Academy. Back then, Steve had just turned 18 and Phil was 20, and they spent the next four years in the same company and graduated together in 1963. Phil was married shortly after graduating from the academy, and the chaplain who performed the wedding ceremony was one of the parish priests when Steve was a boy in Connecticut (to which Steve referenced the six degrees of separation). Steve eventually became the godfather to one of Phil's daughters (Steve joked that he was chosen for that role because of his Sicilian heritage). About the same time, but still unbeknownst to Phil and Steve, Bill had enlisted in the U.S. Air Force and went to a training school to become an aircraft mechanic. He became a crew chief on a C-124 cargo plane and flew throughout Europe and the U.S. before leaving the Air Force in June of 1965, which was followed by classes to receive his FAA–A&E license. He lived in Paris, Munich and London, worked on Department of Commerce Trade exhibits, and even ran with the bulls in Pamplona, Spain, which he said was the scariest thing he had ever done. In the meantime, Phil then began a distinguished 25-year tour in the Navy, which included Vietnam War service and over 1,100 aircraft carrier landings. Shortly after Steve returned back to the states from his tour in Vietnam, he took a trip to Mexico City for the 1968 Olympics with a dozen others. As fate would have it, in the midst of those guys was Bill, whom none of them knew, but whose brother had served in the Marine Corps with some of them. After the memorable trip to Mexico where Bill quickly became a member of the band of brothers, he moved in with Steve for a while in Laguna Beach, and their friendship continued to develop. Bill was working for Tallmantz Aviation as a crew chief on B-25s, and they used 18 of those planes in the movie, "Catch 22", that was being filmed in San Carlos, Mexico (the story goes that Bill broke some of John Wayne's ribs in a fight in a bar there one night, but I never did hear the end of that story). Meanwhile, back in California, Steve began to fly as a pilot for a commercial airline and circled the globe, with stories to tell about far off cities and places that I had certainly never been to. After Bill returned to California from Mexico, he spent his daytime hours employed by the city of Laguna and by the Reef Liquor store at night. After working his way towards positions in the United States Commerce Department and later the State Department, he coordinated projects here, there, and everywhere for some 35 years. To hear Bill talk about his past life, I honestly don't think there's a major city in the world that he has NOT been in at one time or another (kind of boring to think I spent practically my entire 52 years of life residing in one small mid-west city). Steve shared a funny story about how he visited Bill in the Holy Land in 1971, but that everything they did was *not* religious in nature (he said that Tel Aviv was a bit on the wild side). Meanwhile back at the ranch, Phil was then single and attending Harvard Business School in the Navy. In 1972 he moved to Laguna Beach during the summer to hang out with Steve (they kid about it definitely being the "Summer of 72" because a friend of theirs opened and closed a bar during that time period… if the walls could have talked!). In June of 1973, at the age of 32, Steve finally settled down and got married to a wonderful woman named Barb, and Bill returned from one of his far-away-lands to arrange Steve's bachelor's party (which they claimed was an epic event that is still talked about among the mentally ill). Phil came out to California for the wedding with his lady friend, Jan, and after the wedding, Bill went back to whatever foreign land he had flown in from, and Phil and his beloved Jan went back to the east coast and got married. This trio (more like true brothers) continued to cross paths with each other on an intermittent basis for years and never lost contact with each other. According to Steve (the diehard Yankees fan who was wearing his Yankee-"NY" hat that evening), the other two Red Sox fans had to continually mail him a check for lost baseball bets, so they were always in touch (Steve would say that he learned early on to always bet on the Yankees). The years rolled on, and Bill, while traveling the world, somehow arranged to have a house built for him in Laguna Beach in his absence. Since he was now married with two small boys, he would still periodically show up on Laguna Beach's doorstep to visit that side of the country. Phil and Steve would see each other at class reunions and during other planned occasional visits. Since Bill worked in and out of Washington D.C., when Phil returned from the Navy and was living with his wife Jan in Fairfax, those two were then able to hook up with increasing frequency. Steve lost his beloved wife Barb to cancer, but eventually was reacquainted with a lady friend from earlier in his life, Carol ("CT"). Steve and Carol now divide their time between houses in Colorado and California and stay incredibly busy. Upon Bill's retirement from his government service, he began spending his time in his home in Laguna Beach or visiting his girlfriend Lucilla, who resides in D.C. (whom Bill met during an assignment working in Sao Paulo, Brazil). Soon Steve invited Bill to jump on the Habitat for Humanity bandwagon, and the two of them worked together on one of Marilyn's other teams when they built houses in Argentina and Romania. Then last September, when Steve passed through D.C. to visit Phil, they talked about the possibility of an open spot on Marilyn's January/ February Nepal HFH team, and the rest is history. It was an awful lot of fun to be in the company of those three extremely intelligent, quick-witted and humorous men, and I looked forward to hearing more of their stories on this trip. They always enjoyed splitting 650ml bottles of the locally brewed Mt. Everest beer when a cold one was readily available, and at one point during the evening, Bill even jokingly picked up a shiny gold food tray to admire his gorgeous face and smooth down the hairs on his head (never a dull moment). We left the restaurant to head back to the hotel, and somewhere in the darkness of the night in an area void of street lights, Steve tripped over a pole guide wire which was angled and attached at ground level. His sudden fall to the ground scared the behjeeesus out of everybody who went running towards him, but with his cat-like reflexes, he was up in a flash. Luckily, with no permanent damage done to his body, no broken bones, glasses intact, etc., our little traveling band continued onto the hotel where Doc proceeded to supply Steve with some nice antibiotics and guidance for care of the wound on his scraped-up and bloodied shin, etc. (we hadn't even been to the worksite for Day #1 yet, and we had an injury already – haha!). It was so great to have a team doctor along; he had already given drugs to Phil and Cheryl for their colds and stuffiness, too! We all sat around for an hour or so talking and laughing in the icebox hotel lobby (where we got up and continually kept shutting the front door which would swing open without a folded newspaper stuck in the door frame). One by one we slowly drifted to our rooms, but before leaving the lobby I quickly sent Parkview-Tina and my daughter Ab an email, hoping that I had remembered her correct email address since I lost that freakin' journal on Day #2 of the trip! Got upstairs, changed into *warm* winter pajamas, brushed my teeth with bottled water, and then crawled under Mom's rag rug for warmth and settled in for a night of sleep. With my body clock still on Indiana time, it seemed like I slept for about four hours, and then I was wide awake, tossing and turning the rest of the night. So many memories and thoughts ran through my mind during those hours in the stillness of the night, with the rhythm of Deb's breathing from her nearby twin bed as background music. I thought about all of the paths that God had led me down, and the blessings that followed. I had a childhood that others were envious of, with great parents and memories of fun family

25

vacations and loving experiences to last me a lifetime. That family bond would become the love that I would mold my own family around, as I fell in love and got married to a wonderful man, Doug Donaldson, shortly out of high school, and our two super children followed. I loved being a stay-at-home mom, and then when the kids were both in school, I began to work as the assistant to the plant manager at Cooper Engineered Products, an automotive supplier in Auburn. The years rolled by, and Alex and Abby quickly grew into teenagers and life became stressful (I would guess that for most parents, when your kids become teenagers, that is an understatement). No one ever begins a marriage thinking you'll be divorced someday, and one of my real regrets in life is that I didn't work hard enough on our marriage, which ended in divorce in 1997 (Life-Awakening-#1). I don't think I will ever forgive *myself* for not trying harder for all four of us. Period. In the years that followed, I developed new friendships and fell in and out of love with some good men and have great memories and photograph albums that help me re-live those crazy times. I bought my own home in Auburn, made close friends with my neighbors, and watched as my children grew into talented, compassionate young adults. Alex and Ashley were married in the spring of 2003, and Abby was busy with a part-time job while going to college in Fort Wayne. Later that fall, after our family lost my beloved brother-in-law, Randy, in a tragic auto accident, I began to see life like never before. When riding on the back of a motorcycle with one of my beaus, I started to notice every single hawk and bird sitting on every fence post, and almost felt like I could see every blade of grass in my backyard. I began to see and feel the emotions and the struggles in life that people were facing, more than I noticed their clothing, job title, or tangible items. In 2006, my first grandchild, Baylie, made her entrance into the world, and I began the wonderful journey of grandparenthood! Shortly thereafter, I sold my house and left my job in the automotive world to follow a jaded love into the private business sector, which left me homeless, jobless, and loveless when it all fell apart (that period in my life also racked up the still-standing family record of moving all of my enough-to-fill-a-3-bedroom-home-earthly possessions four different times within an 11-month timeframe). Thank God I had my ever-supportive family and Cooper buds, Tom and Rex, who moved Flossie and me and all of my crapola, and put up with me during that insane year. Both of my sisters (Carol and Becky) and their families were godsends, and Becky truly kept me from going nuts by offering to let me and Floss live in the finished basement of her home for several months while I got my feet back underneath me. That depressive feeling of unemployment and not having a place to call my own was something I had never experienced before. I suddenly had a real-life understanding and concept of what those hardships meant to the countless thousands in the world that struggled to find their true self during tough times. With the help of a gifted human-resources friend, Bruce Buttermore, I eventually began working for an automotive sorting company. With a job in place, I had the opportunity to move back to Auburn (the city where I had previously lived every single minute of my entire life prior to my 11-month-nutsville-period). One of my past-beloved beaus, Mike Gerig, was looking for someone to rent the house next door to him, which was owned by his father, Norm, who was moving into a nursing home. To the hallelujahs of my moving-day family and friends and my dog, Flossie, (who had become petrified every time I pulled out the Vera Bradley overnight bag), moving into Norm's vacated house would be the final time we would relocate all of my possessions during the fateful year of 2006. What a relief to be back in Auburn and living in such a great neighborhood. God was slowly piecing the whole puzzle of my life together again and I was tagging along like clockwork (I am so thankful He lets us patch over some of our stupid mistakes and provides the glue of forgiveness). Eventually I bought that little white house which was a real privilege to live where Norm had lived, and it quickly became home. Every time I held my growing granddaughter, it was an affirmation to me that life was good and it would be all right again. My mom once told me that she thought that one's life went in slow motion until the minute you graduated from high school or college and hit the reality of the world and from them on, life, in her view, had flown by at breakneck speed. At the time she said that, I didn't believe her. But through the years I had now found that to be true of my own life. My granddaughter was growing like a weed, and time seemed to now be flying by. In the spring of 2007, I was again blessed to follow HR Bruce into the healthcare industry, where we both began working at PLH. It was there that I learned the real meaning of compassionate care and serving others, and the heart behind the "why" of "what we do" in healthcare (Life-Awakening-#2). I was fortunate to assist a sharp, young COO, Rob Myers, who let me spread my wings and absorb some patient-contact service-excellence work within the realm of my administrative duties, and my days spent at that little hospital quickly became my life's passion. To me, there wasn't anything more gratifying than to be able to reassure someone that they would receive excellent care during their hospital stay, and then following up with them to make sure they knew you were there for them. The staff in that hospital was like my second family, and even though it was a long drive from Auburn to LaGrange each day, I truly felt like that was where God wanted me to be. I remember telling Rob that with all of the wonderful things I witnessed daily within our Parkview walls, shame on me if I couldn't find the time to write a thank-you note *each day* and mail it. I put my money where my mouth was, and in 2009, I made a personal goal for myself to hand-write and mail 365 thank-you notes to our PLH staff. By the end of the year, I cleared that goal with ease (Quint Studer would have been so proud of me!). In the last weeks of 2009, I accepted a position assisting two executives at the Parkview Corporate Office in Fort Wayne, and I quickly fell into the mind-boggling pace of the executive world. Even though I missed the patient contact, working in Fort Wayne ended up being a life-changing move for me as the reduced drive time added a whole extra hour of free time into my life, every single work day. I was challenged and inspired by some of the most passionate, humorous and witty executives I had ever been around, and after a couple of months I was soon spending every day solely assisting Rick Henvey, our Parkview Regional COO, one of the most talented multi-taskers I had ever worked with. With the birth of my grandson in 2010, our new Gage, and his sister Baylie, continued to add a new generation of love into our family and life was, as my mom had predicted, moving by at breakneck speed. I was really sensing that if you stood still and took anything for granted, it seemed to be very possible that you could miss out on all of the simple, treasured moments in life. Every time I stood still long enough to look back over my shoulder, I could easily see the path that God had led me down. Makes me laugh at myself, thinking I always know what's best for me, when it's really God that keeps picking me up, brushing me off, and pointing me in the right direction, time and time again. Looking back, I had fallen in and out of love countless times, been unemployed and living in my sister's basement, and at the darkest point of my life where I wasn't sure I could go on, God had led me smack dab into the compassionate world of health care, which changed my life in unimaginable ways. My goal was to try to live each day of my life, as Matthew Kelly would say, as the best version of me. There really wasn't any physical adventure I wasn't scared to pursue, and in the 51st year of my life, some people began to think I had lost my marbles when within a matter of months I made two adventurous separate climbs up two 200+ foot tower cranes on our hospital's regional build site, rode in a 25-mile bike race mid-summer, and then completed a tandem parachute jump out of a perfectly good airplane with a handful of Parkview co-workers. I seemed to have hurdled right past the events of that summer, and those pieces of my life-puzzle got snapped into place (with my younger sister Becky quipping, "You know you don't have to complete your entire bucket list all in one year."). I kept tossing and turning in that tiny little freezing cold twin bed in Kathmandu, and throughout all of those things running through my head, I had this overwhelming vision that writing a book was going to be the next piece of the puzzle of my life. Would people think I was nuts if I said that out loud? Was I the only one that felt like it seemed that life was just one big puzzle, and the further we got into the puzzle, and the more pieces of it we had figured out, the quicker we came to finishing the puzzle? Does life seem to move faster the older we get and we start to figure out the meaning of life and are somehow able to see the roads we are led down? Was that possibly the reason that God had led me to say yes to come on this trip with Marilyn and her team to Nepal? Although it did occur on me that I really didn't know anything about writing a book, how to find a publisher or any of that, I still felt in those early morning hours in that freezing cold hotel room in Kathmandu, that if writing a book was what God wanted to challenge me with next, it would happen. I let my thoughts drift back to one of those wonderful loves in my life, and pretended his strong arms were tightly wrapped around my body, drawing me in close to help me stop shivering, and I finally drifted off to sleep.

Chapter 4

Monday, January 17, 2011

We woke up early, went downstairs and ate breakfast in the hotel dining room. We then met Manish, the Nepal HFH coordinator, and another gentleman, one of their HFH "big wigs" for the district. They explained to us about our mission for the next two weeks, and answered a lot of questions we had about how the home-building process functioned in Nepal. He shared info on the families' sweat equity on the project, and how the two families we would be building homes with had been saving money for their homes thru a micro-financing company that assisted people in Third World countries to afford housing, etc. He said our two families outside of Biratnagar had continually "grown in stature" by learning to save, learning to read, etc. (most of the families working with HFH had been illiterate, but were now taking classes to become literate). He said in many areas of Nepal there was "no free education", so if a family was poor, they couldn't send their children to school, therefore no one in the family ever learned to read. Building each home would cost approximately $1500 USD, with each family providing the equivalent of $300 of that amount. He shared that these families would also invest 300–1000 sweat equity hours on their own home (and after looking back and remembering how hard the families worked beside us each day, I have no doubt in that whatsoever). He said that each day, HFH was currently working on houses for five different families throughout the country, and their goal was to eventually help seven to ten families a day, which would mean 100,000 new homes within the next five years in Nepal. Wow. They were currently building incremental model houses, starting out with two rooms and a veranda, (or two rooms with an indoor toilet) and most families chose the veranda option for the social aspect, rather than to build a home with a bathroom (since they had lived their entire lives up to this point without indoor plumbing). After their home was paid off in three years, each family then had the option to add on another room (or the bathroom). He told us that our financial donation would go to help build houses for close to 15 families in one form or another (we paid a $500 donation up front when we joined the Global Village Habitat for Humanity work team). The HFH coordinators had just come from the eastern part of Nepal, where the village living conditions were even worse than they were in Biratnagar. He said it was not uncommon to find several families and their animals, (which often included men, women, children, cow, water buffalo and bull), all living in one area (that was about the size of the icebox hotel lobby we were then sitting in wearing two layers of clothing to stay warm). The two families that we would be helping in the coming days started by applying and meeting with members of lending groups, where they were taught to save and were involved in making plans for the building of their future homes. The coordinators were so thankful that we had come to help HFH in their beloved Nepal, and in his closing remarks, in broken limited English, one of them said, *"Lots of exciting, many courage."* I loved that, and thought that should be our team motto for the week (especially at that point, since we had no idea what lay ahead of us during our 11 days of riding in the bus with Dependra). Led by Puskal, our team all jumped in a Raya Tours long extended van, and went to visit Babukaji and Bungamati, two older, smaller villages outside of Kathmandu that were adjoined by walkways and terraced gardens. It was such a wonderful cultural experience, wandering along stone streets, bordered on each side by three-story ancient brick buildings, with window openings draped by strings of dried peppers to ward off evil spirits. There were little wooden door entrances into adjoined brick structures where people lived all around us, and it was a real warm-hearted feeling being enveloped in their neighborhood village streets. We mingled in among the local families, and took some wonderful pictures, and were always greeted with a prayerful-hand-clasped "Namaste" (a Hindu greeting). Along one uneven, cracked stone pathway we came upon this big white chicken, with what appeared to be eight little chicks hidden beneath her feathers, with their 16 little chicken feet exposed below her feathery-wing-expanded protective body. As we all stopped to take a picture of this protective mother chicken with 18 feet, out of a nearby doorway ran this little village woman, with a frightened face, thinking that we were about to steal her beloved fat hen and hidden chicks. When she quickly realized we strangers weren't wanting to steal her chicken, but were only snapping a quick picture of her feathered flock, she smiled and proceeded to quickly scoop up the mother hen and all of the scattering chicks into her long scarf and apron that adorned her well-worn and tattered dress. The terraced gardens and rice fields were amazing, and during the hour walk on brick-lined pathways in the morning fog, this whole village seemed ancient and mystical (until that morning walk, places like those villages only existed in my imagination). We walked through one temple area in Bungamati, with century-old concrete Buddha figurines and lion statues that protected temple worshipping areas that seemed to be wearing away from bird poop or years of pollution-decay. Doc stirred up some neighborhood dogs, and I thought they were going to have him for lunch! We climbed back in the van and drove back into Kathmandu for lunch, where we had the most wonderful "pea soup" (which I think might have had only two peas in it, but it tasted more like Campbell's tomato soup with lots of gooey melted cheese on top, it was yummy). Our next stop was the Kathmandu airport, where we would take a flight to another portion of Nepal where the HFH build would take place in a village community. As the van pulled up to the airport departure drop-off area, this led to another interesting experience with our team unloading all of our luggage from the top of the Raya Tours van, and quickly being surrounded by Nepalese men offering to carry our bags for "dollar, dollar", pushing towards us, etc. We just ignored them and carried our own stuff, which had Doc laughing because with his camera strapped around his neck and loaded down with luggage, he said he was really feeling like a Japanese tourist at that moment. We told Puskal good-bye and that we would see him in eleven days after our HFH build. We waited an hour or two, and then caught a flight out of Kathmandu on Buddha Air (I knew Buttermore would love that one) headed to Biratnagar. While we were flying over snowy Himalayan mountaintops, I sat beside Bill and fired up Doc's Notebook on the short flight (I gratefully had accepted his offer to use his electronic device to journal the trip, after losing my paper journal, dang it!). It amazed me to sit in a seat on a flight beside somebody who had spent their entire career flying around the world; while I was continually in awe of looking out the window or slightly nervous when the aircraft would leave the ground or pitch or sway in mid-flight, these three experienced pilots on our team would either be reading or snoozing or not having a care in the world about the flight. I realized if they weren't worried, I shouldn't be either (but you could be sure that if I saw them looking around, then I'd be paying attention too). I proceeded to save a test document on the Notebook prior to starting the journal, and about the time I had that done, the "please store all electronic equipment" message was being delivered in a language I didn't understand, and the 45-minute flight was over and we were landing in Biratnagar. The lack of security in that airport was immediately evident. As we were rolling down the landing strip after touchdown while circling back to the airport, we passed several groups of ladies standing near the edge of the runway, cutting down tall grass with long machetes. We were met at the airport by Rajesh Rai, the local HFH coordinator, who would also become our translator and tour guide during the home-builds, and "Dancing" a HFH volunteer, who adorned our necks with beautiful welcoming necklaces made of strung-together marigolds. I had to giggle because as they were making these presentations of welcome, all 11 of our team members were trying to grab our American/ Mexican luggage off of the conveyor belt rollers before it walked away in the hands of those Nepalese folks we had just arrived with. When we reached our HFH bus, our team stood behind a banner that Rajesh had made, which read "Habitat for Humanity Nepal, Global Village Program, U.S. Team, 17–27 January 2011". As soon as we were done taking the picture, Rajesh, Dancing, and the bus driver, Dependra, tied the banner onto the side of the bus for a little free HFH advertisement as we were transported into Biratnagar. After a short ride through chaotic traffic-packed streets, we pulled up in front of the Ratna Hotel, which would become home base for our HFH team for the next almost-two-weeks. We all entered the hotel lobby, and Marilyn called out room assignments: I would be sharing Room 407 with Linda Patterson. Linda worked at PLH along with Marilyn as a nurse in the Emergency Department, and I knew that rooming with Linda would be a lot of fun. We climbed up several flights of stairs in search of Room 407, which we thought should be 307, as wherever we went in Nepal, the rooms were not numbered according to the same "floor system" that we have in the States. Our room had two twin beds and a window that overlooked the metropolis of the approximately 900,000 residents that called Biratnagar home (big city). When we looked past the curtains, there was hardly green-to-be-seen anywhere, except a patch of grass in a yard behind the hotel, and a few scattered palm trees in the neighborhood amidst the overcast sky. We unpacked a few things and quickly went about checking out the room and noticing the difference in our cultures. We still had not found hot water on this trip yet, and in each of the hotel room bathrooms we had encountered so far, the entire bathroom was a tiled shower area (when you attempted to take a shower, the water spray went EVERYWHERE in the bathroom, hence the tile-everything). They had no concept of shower curtains whatsoever, and neither bathroom had any kind of tub enclosure, either. It always made taking a shower an act of magic, as you had to pre-plan where to put your clean clothes and dry towel as to not soak them during the shower process. Another trick to deal with was the electricity, as the electrical power ceased to exist at multiple times each day in the city, so the generators (hopefully) continued to kick off and on. The room key was also used as a mechanism to turn on the electricity to the room, so the minute that you'd pull the room key out of the slot on the wall to leave the room, all of the power would shut off (so much for charging our cameras or the Notebook while we were out of the room!). After settling in, we had a short break and then went downstairs where Rajesh, Dancing, and two other representatives from the local corporate sponsor of this mission spoke to us, and shared how the project had progressed. I had trouble staying awake during their presentation which took place in a board room at the hotel, which looked like it was pseudo decorated 77 years ago. The room was lined with cut bamboo wall covering and crude electrical outlets, and light fixtures sporadically hung in weird unexplainable places. They appeared to be so proud and honored to have visiting Americans, and the tables were set up in a U-shape arrangement and covered with white tablecloths (which looked they had been used by several groups prior to us) and red table skirts. We were there for maybe an hour, and then we broke up and took a quick nap before coming back downstairs around 7:00pm for dinner. That dinner, and every subsequent meal here served to us in the hotel during the morning or evening hours for the next 11 days, was served buffet style, with many different dishes. I ate a lot of rice and pita bread, and French fries (I decided I was going to be starch queen at the end of two weeks if everything remained that spicy). I made a pact with myself that the following night I was going to ask them for butter and sugar, and I would end up eating rice just like I did back home on occasion! We had lots of fun at dinner, and I quickly sensed that our team was comprised of amazing people, who had previously been on COUNTLESS Habitat work trips around the *entire globe*. I sat by Deb, Cheryl and Larry, and enjoyed getting to know Larry and Cheryl a little more, while hearing about their farm in Benton County, Indiana. They have adult children just like me; a daughter and a son slightly older than my two children, with granddaughters (and were buying lots of pink John Deere accessories for them), and even a new granddaughter that was born after they left to travel to Nepal! During dinner Phil choked on a hot green pepper in some of the spicy food, and he couldn't catch his breath for a few minutes; his face was red, eyes watering, etc. It was very comforting to know that we had Doc, Marilyn and Linda with us who were definitely more medically and clinically skilled than the rest of our team should anything happen to us. On the way back upstairs from dinner, I forgot that I had unzipped my backpack to get out a pen, and my backpack slipped off of my shoulder. My birth control pills, that I was taking specifically for this trip so I wasn't feeling like I could fly kites and ride bikes during the Himalayan trek where bathroom facilities would be minimal, spewed out of my backpack and slid across the floor of the hotel lobby. One of the over-attentive bellboys ran over, grabbed the pill disk from the floor with this very inquisitive look on his face, and then handed them back to me. AGH!! I ran upstairs hoping to get a shower before the hot water was gone for the day, but no such luck, not a drop of hot or even warm water. Bummer. So Linda and I called the desk and asked for extra blankets, and I quickly found that my head was bobbing while trying to type into the trip journal, so we both quickly crashed. Around 3:00am, I woke up and could NOT go back to sleep. My wide-awake and inquiring mind wanted to know: *How long does it take to flip your mind and body to the*

Third World time zone anyway??? I thought to myself..., I'll be quiet and sneak to the bathroom in the dark as to not wake up Linda..., so I snuck into the bathroom on that cold, solid tile floor, which was still soaking wet from my first attempt to take a shower in there before bedtime (back when I found there was ZERO hot water and the water was freezing, but that still had left the entire bathroom floor wet and very slick!). So there I was, middle of the night, in my long pajama pants, trying to walk and not fall on my butt, holding up my pant legs and squatting on the toilet (yes, thank God, at least in the Ratna we still had western toilets). Have you ever tried to hold up your pajama pants, wipe your girlie parts, pull your pants back up, and not let any piece of clothing hit the wet floor? When I had succeeded in all of the above, I climbed back into bed, but then I was wide awake. Then a thought suddenly popped into my head, "What the heck, I'm gonna get up and see if I can find the Notebook and my glasses in the dark and continue on with the journal!" Since I couldn't remember where I had left any of those necessary and important objects (Notebook, glasses, etc.) and it was **pitch black** as I was lying on my stomach, I quietly felt around on the nightstand in between Linda and myself. I found a pair of glasses, but after I put them on, I realized they were my SUNGLASSES, so I shoved my head facedown in the pillow and proceeded to laugh out loud in the pillow at the thought of myself, lying on a very hard twin bed in Nepal, under many heavy blankets trying to stay warm, in the dark of night, now wearing my sunglasses. It was hilarious. I finally quietly climbed out of bed, and was able to feel around on the floor beside my bed, where BONUS, I was able to find the Notebook, open it up, and use it as a flashlight to locate my glasses! As I proceeded to (again) sneak into the bathroom to sit in the dark and type, I heard Linda snore, so I felt proud that I had survived the obstacle course to reach the bathroom, successful that I hadn't awakened her during this spy adventure. I felt so blessed and emotional right then and there, sitting on that tile floor, typing in the dark. How did Little Kaysie ever get there? It was surreal that I was sitting in Nepal on a bathroom floor with no lighting, listening to a lone dog barking somewhere in the distance, with the occasional sound of honking cars/trucks going by outside (I laughed while thinking to myself, "they are *still* driving like maniacs at 3 o'clock in the morning!"). I looked up and noticed there was a four inch circular hole in the upper corner of the bathroom where a pipe came in from the outside wall, so you could easily hear everything going on outside of the hotel. I felt thankful that I was able to find a dry spot on the tile floor to sit my little butt on, yoga-style with the Notebook in my lap. My knees were soon starting to shake from the cold room, so I mentally made preparations for the future nights and for my next midnight journaling adventure, to plan ahead with a warm rug to sit on and more clothing to battle the cold night air! I quietly opened the bathroom door and grabbed the towel off of the door handle to fold and slide under my butt so I could continue typing without turning into a winter-pajama-clothed frozen popsicle. I already knew of several things I had forgotten or couldn't locate in my luggage: 1) I had left my watch at home – STUPID MOVE, 2) I knew I had packed a plastic soap box, as I had unwrapped a bar of soap and put it somewhere to be packed with my other toiletries when I left Auburn, so since I had yet to find it, I was snickering that Mom had probably found that soap box and was laughing back home, knowing I had forgotten it, and 3) I knew I had packed a flashlight, but couldn't locate that yet either. Other than that, I felt pretty well set clothes-wise, and would continue to wing it for the weeks ahead. I missed Flossie and Mabel sleeping on my bed with me at night, and after I shared that thought with everybody last night during dinner, my team then offered to have Bill come sleep on the foot of my bed in Mabel's place, which made everybody laugh. I knew we had requested a wake up call for 6:30am, but by then it was after 4:00am and it was still pretty freakin' dark outside the bathroom four-inch-hole in the wall. I couldn't wait for daylight to arrive and the first day of HFH work to begin, to see the worksite and figure out how we would be able to help these families. To hear Rajesh describe it, it sounded like we would be making bamboo/mud walls for the homes, with pre-cut bamboo strips which we would weave and then mud over to make walls. I finally convinced myself I was too cold to stay in the bathroom typing in the dark much longer, so I turned off the Notebook and quietly snuck back into my bed in the dark. Felt like I was back at 4-H camp all over again.

Chapter 5

Tuesday, January 18, 2011

Well, after being up long before the crack of dawn, what a great day this was. I started the day with taking the Notebook and heading down three flights of red stinky carpeted stairs to the lobby and paying 200 rps for an hour's worth of Internet connection (the equivalent of about $2.80 USD). At least I was able to drop a couple of emails to people, but was still frustrated because I couldn't get on Facebook, even after I reset my password (but I was totally impressed that the Facebook system recognized that I was signing in from a different country than what I usually did, so it paused and asked me for security clearance for that – haha). We had a GREAT breakfast, the best one yet. We then grabbed our gear, loaded up the "team bus" and headed out to the worksite for Day #1. *Holy crapola,* that bus ride was probably the top adventure of the trip so far. Each detail of that 18-kilometer, 45-minute ride seems to be forever etched in my mind, and yet I still can't find a string of words to adequately describe it to anybody who didn't experience it. I quickly learned that riding in a vehicle, anywhere in Nepal, could be both life-changing and life-ending in the flick of a wrist. Our driver for the duration of the Habitat build, Dependra, appeared to know this area extremely well and navigated the rickety bus through traffic with the talents of a stealth bomber. The insanity of the traffic seemed to be a step more chaotic than Kathmandu (how could *that* be?). I had never seen such madness, with vehicles, human beings, bicycle rickshaws and live animals all trying to survive in the same rolling motion, which was usually delivered to you head-on at breakneck speed. Our first stop was the Biratnagar-equivalent of an American liquor store, where Rajesh jumped off the bus and returned with umpteen cases of purified bottled water for volunteer drinking water at the worksite and cooking water for lunch preparation. The bus itself was enough to giggle over, with incense burning on the dashboard, long fringe adorning the area above the driver's head, and maroon and beige colored velour material throughout the bus. It was sometimes hilarious to look around and see the fringe and everything not hammered down swaying out of control when Dependra was weaving through traffic, with everyone hanging on to the seat frame in front of us, and riding along on unevenly padded seats that would often break through the seat frame and throw you aside. Our next stop was Rajesh's church, where we had to pick up all of the supplies for the on-site build lunches, which would be served to us at a HFH work area near a local school on tables and plastic chairs under a pavilion, maybe a 15-minute walk from the build site. The minister's wife, Jemima, and other church members would be compassionately volunteering their time in the coming days to prepare the daily lunch meal for our entire team, so we formed a water brigade line to move all of the needed supplies (including a propane tank) from their church to street-side where we loaded the bus. I had already learned that "Namaste" was a Hindu greeting, but the greeting for a Christian believer was, "Jaimaiche" (pronounced Jay-ma-shee, which means "Jesus is Lord"), and so that is how we greeted Jemima and the other church members for the duration of our visit, as they were fellow Christians. This 45-minute trip from the city to the worksite was definitely, by far, the most interesting traffic docket that we had experienced yet, with the ride passing many farm animals as we crossed a bridge and left the outskirts of town, and headed out into the countryside. After the bridge, you would have thought we had entered a time warp and had shifted even further back in time, to when gasoline vehicles hadn't been invented yet, and crude roadways and paths were covered with massive oxen teams taking up the width of the road pulling big-wheeled carts, hauling stacks of bamboo or tons of grain, all the while being driven by a Nepalese farmer with a smile on his face ☺. Doc was right when he had described one of his previous trips to Nepal; these really were some of the kindest and gentlest people you would ever want to meet. That particular morning I happened to be sitting behind Rajesh on the bus when we nearly came to a grinding halt because of an adorable little mule, standing right in the middle of the road, trying to eat something off of the mud-covered street. It cracked me up when in his twisted English, Rajesh started laughing and said, "Donkey in the road eating cow dung!" Rajesh reminded me of Tattoo on Fantasy Island, "Da plane, da plane"; his tone of voice was exactly the same, and he was always amused by himself. I was amazed at how well some of the people we came in contact with could translate their language to English so quickly (I could certainly never whip sentences together like that in a foreign language, even after taking two years of Senora Smith's Spanish class at DeKalb High School). We kept passing what reminded me of Abby's famous Christmas-time-created chocolate-dipped pretzel rods, standing vertical against fences, but instead Rajesh explained that they were what almost every village family living outside of the city made to create their own fuel to fix their meals over the fire with: they were rows of leftover thin weed rods, mashed together *by hand* with straw and fresh cow dung, then handcrafted to stand about five feet high, and all lined up to dry (they would eventually be cut, lit on fire, and used for cooking heat material – could you imagine how that would smell up a living area that had little-or-no ventilation??? Wooowee!). We continued on for what seemed like forever, winding down these country paths, over EXTREMELY bumpy roads that I thought our bus would not be capable of traversing, past fields of sugar cane, rice, mustard seed, cauliflower and cabbage, with many workers in field rows harvesting their crops (I kept thinking I was just having a dream and had ended up in a National Geographic magazine somewhere). We had to turn around several times because of blocked roadways with other big wagons or broken-down vehicles, but eventually we made our way outside of the village of Kamalpur, to one of the government schools near the build site where we would be served lunch each day. We dropped the cooks and the kitchen supplies off, and it was there where I experienced my first practice shot at urinating over an official squat toilet, nothing but a hole in the middle of a ceramic flat tile on the floor, with usually two small buckets nearby… one bucket that remained empty into which you would deposit your used toilet paper, the other bucket usually contained water to rinse off the ceramic when you were done (and you weren't surprised if you didn't have either of those buckets on occasion, either). I was laughing out loud while doing it, as I then believed that we women just weren't fashioned to "go" in this position: it was hard to pee while you were squatting and laughing at the same time, but I prevailed! It was cool seeing everybody carrying supplies towards the worksite while walking along a narrow path in between two sugar cane fields. We eventually came to a clearing where the road curved and there was the Promised Land, with a big field of green winter wheat in the foreground – the area where the homes would soon be built. We looked ahead and there were the two bamboo-framed stick house frame structures rising from the ground and part of the mud floors already in place, recently formed by a HFH pre-construction team. Wow, after dreaming about this for months, it was so cool to see that it had become reality. This community was made up of very poor people who built their houses with mud floors, thatched roofs, and mud walls without proper ventilation. There was no proper sanitation, and not a lot of clean drinking water facilities, although you would occasionally see a pump on someone's property. The men made their living through daily wage labor in a nearby city

44

or farming, and the women sometimes helped the family through domestic work, animal rearing, or by working small odd jobs within the villages. Their families' monthly incomes were basically around $84.00 per month. Rajesh led us to an area in front of the two current homes of these families (that looked like thatch covered buildings on Gilligan's Island, except their roofs had squash vines growing on them). It was strange to see all of the villagers staring at the Americans and Felix, our beloved "MexiNepalese" (which is what Felix had lovingly started calling himself, since with his Mexican skin tone, people kept thinking he was a local Nepali). We had a little ceremony where we met the two home partner families, and they presented us with flower leis to show their welcome and appreciation. In this culture, the women seemed to be the head of the household, and it just so happened that we were building houses for two families, in which the wives were sisters. House #1 would be built for the older sister, 35-year old Bagabati Singh and her family, which was made up of her husband, Rajindar, and two sons Umesh and Ramesh, and a daughter Ranju. House #2 would be built for her younger sister, Amala Devi (age 30), and her husband, Ram Babu, and their two daughters, Anita and Babita, and a son, Dashrath. With many sets of village eyes upon us, we quickly set off to divide up into two teams (one for each house), with workers either preparing the bamboo by cutting off the bamboo joints on the approximately 1.5" wide split pieces to make them smooth and pliable, or measuring how long to cut the pieces that needed to be woven into the slat-framed house walls. Our teams had a lot of fun working together and talking non-stop that morning, the sun eventually brightened up the overcast haze, and I got sunburned on my lily-white-Hoosier face. The families and the entire community seemed very excited and inquisitive to see exactly what we were doing there and the process we would use to build these houses. They spent a lot of time just standing around and staring at us, especially the smaller children. All of the residents of this village had dark skin and beautiful dark hair, and there we were, Milquetoast white folks. With Phil and me sporting reddish hair, they continued to stare at us to try and figure us out. Other than some of the HFH house framers and Rajesh, no one spoke any English, so there wasn't a lot of communication except for hand gestures or smiles. All of us quickly learned how to get our point across without words; it was like an instantaneous Mime 101 class (nor did anyone understand a lot of English, either). I continued to be lost when they tried to tell me words, as they rrrrrrrrollled their r's and some of their first names were SO LONG (to remember). We all thought it was cute when nine-year old Dashrath chased down his billy goat because apparently his mom told him that she didn't want the goat to eat the sugar cane leaves by their house. It was funny, because even though we couldn't comprehend any of what they were saying, you could usually pick up on what was going on just by watching what was happening around us. When Dashrath finally caught up with the little black and white goat and grabbed him, I asked if I could hold his goat. He handed him over to me, and the village crowd laughed at me holding their goat, it was very funny. From that moment on, Linda started referring to this particular black and white goat as Bob, and we would always call him "Ba-ah-ah-ah-ahbbb", like the sound that Bob always made. We quickly had several bamboo sections completed on both houses, and then we broke for lunch and took the 15-minute walk back over to the government school to the area we used for our daily lunches. The wife of Rajesh's minister, Jemima (her English name), and PooPoo (which meant sister) and their church friends made us a fabulous lunch. We had all worked very hard that morning and so we were really grateful for a chance to sit down for the lunch break and rest our aching bodies (this Habitat for Humanity stuff was going to be a good workout!). We all got a big chuckle out of Deb saying that she loved the little fried-pork-loin-looking chips, so that's what we all assumed they were, until Rajesh overheard us talking and told us they were crawfish. Knowing that Deb HATED seafood, Doc and everybody started laughing, and so they brought out an empty box that the prawns had been in, and showed the box to Deb. Out of disbelief, Deb took her reading glasses out of her backpack and read the ingredients on the side of the package, which had us cracking up! Linda and I threw a few of our leftover lunch scraps to this stray dog that had wandered over to the lunch tables and spent the entire lunch staring at us. The dog had the same loving eyes as my black Lab back in the States, so from them on, we referred to this stray as "Mabel". This Nepalese-Mabel was built like a smooth collie with a black face, light brown muzzle, brown patches above each eye, with a black body and four white legs. She was *so thin* that her rib and hip bones protruded through her hide, and she appeared to have a litter of pups hidden somewhere, as her tits were huge and sagging. She was very untrusting of us and would never get close when we called her. When we told her she was a "good girl", we got a quick tail wag, but she would still not come near. The enclosed squat toilet was about 50 yards from our lunch break area, so if we had a need, we would visit the outhouse while we were there for lunch, prior to heading back to the worksite (I think the guys usually took the liberty of using the nearby sugar cane field... traitors). The pavilion area where we ate our lunches was near a bamboo processing station. There, they would work on the cut bamboo, as it was soaked in big vats of boric acid for 24 hours and then laid out to be dried and cut. A bamboo-splitting tool that reminded us of a big apple corer, was hammered onto the end of a rod of bamboo, and was then pulled and pounded through the entire rod of bamboo (which looked like pieces of string cheese as the bamboo was split). This splitting and pounding generated the 1.5" wide pieces of bamboo that we were trimming at the worksite. It was interesting to see this in action, as it helped me better understand the process of the bamboo to get it to the condition of the pieces that we were handling, which eventually would be woven into the open sections on the houses. We finished up lunch and walked back to the worksite, where the crowd of interested onlookers continued to grow throughout the first afternoon of work. I enjoyed working side by side with Amala's youngest 11-year old daughter Babita, as we sat on small stools and trimmed bamboo pieces. She was a beautiful young girl, with long dark hair pulled back in a pink-checkered scarf. She wore a small thin gold ring through her left nostril, and her eyes were gorgeous. I kept thinking she could have easily been a model. She didn't know any English but seemed to understand what we would motion to her, and she continually smiled while staring at us. By the time the two village schools let out around 4:00pm, we had a huge audience of gawkers. I'm sure word was spreading quickly about the foreign people that they were calling "artists" in their language, who had come from America to help build these two homes in their community. I took lots of pictures that afternoon during a break, and enjoyed capturing shots of all of the school children intensely watching Larry, Cheryl, and Phil weaving inside of Bagabati's house. Larry had his tape measure attached to his jeans, and while Phil was weaving, Larry would measure the next bamboo piece for a correct length. Amazingly, the HFH pre-construction team had rigged up crude electricity to the worksite so that they could use power tools to create the bamboo house frames. With limited power during the day, Larry would use his carried-from-America electric saw to cut the bamboo. I'm sure the children were in awe at that monster-machine that was chewing up the bamboo, and at the tall, strongly-built Indiana-farmer-man wearing a baseball cap and a big smile, that was making it work. Doc and Bill were weaving away on Amala's house, and they were using a hacksaw to cut their bamboo, which Doc was using with the precision of one of his surgical scalpels back at the hospital. The children were so precious, and I soon taught young Dashrath and his buddies how to give a knuckle bump, which they thought was odd and funny. It was hard to remember their names, and it made me realize when I met someone new back in the States, I often used the memory trick of associating their name with the name of someone I already knew, to trigger a recall mechanism in my brain. However, when I met these people in this Nepalese village that had six syllables in their first name, I was stumped to use the same memory tool. I started to write their names in a paper pad that I kept in my backpack, and Dependra (our bus driver) spoke fairly good English, so we began to use him for an interpreter too. In the afternoons, Dependra would often come to the worksite and work beside us after he helped clean up after our lunch meal over on the school grounds. He explained to us that he tried to watch movies in English to help him conquer our English language, and then he rattled off names like "the Governor", Arnold Schwarzenegger, Angelina Jolie, Brad Pitt, Tom Cruise, etc. I was stunned when he shared with us in his broken English that he knew all about "the sadness of your country's 9/11 tragedy", and how much it had affected our nation. It was very touching to hear him say that. It made me reflect on the fact that I knew basically nothing about Nepal other than the few geographic/demographic blurbs I had read about the country, and yet there was our bus driver, telling me all of the things that he knew about America. We continued splitting bamboo and filling up the open sections on the walls of the houses, with a tea break in the afternoon, and we wrapped up around 5:00pm by storing all our tools back into a HFH tool box which would be left onsite each day. What an eventful ride back to the hotel, as it seemed to mirror the disbelief factor from the morning trip. We had to slow to a stop to make way for a tractor/wagon pulling heavy sand, and when the tractor driver jerked to take off to move around our bus on the narrow roadway, his entire HEAVY load came unhitched from his tractor, tipping the loaded wagon back and off of the ball of the hitch, leaving him stranded. Luckily, Milan ("Mee-lan"), Dependra's driving assistant, was able to move some bamboo barriers along the road which enabled us to pass by (or we would have been there for hours). Milan truly did have a big job on the bus, as it was his responsibility to rapidly *BANG LOUDLY* on the bus door that he precariously hung on to and outside of, to alert Dependra when the bus was clear of any obstacles. He was often leaping out the bus door to run ahead and clear the path for our bus through stalled traffic, and he seemed to be an expert at shooing away stray goats, or ducks and chickens that were often in our path on the roads, etc. It was cute, while driving through one village neighborhood that afternoon, we all laughed when we saw a young boy running down the road in front of our bus, enjoying the simple thrill of rolling a bicycle tire along with a stick, just like some of us did when we were children (although in our high-tech society, we hadn't seen any children do that in a long time). We got back to the hotel in one piece – wow, we had survived Day #1 (the ride to and from the worksite held a much greater chance of getting injured than did working at the home site). We all met downstairs in the conference room of the Ratna for dinner at 7:00pm, which seemed to be a repeat of Dinner #1, and we all joked in good humor that it would probably be the same choices of dinner selections for the next 11 days. When we all parted after the meal, I went back upstairs to our room and finally got a hot shower, which felt SO GOOD (through Larry's detective work, we finally figured out that our hot water heater hadn't been turned on... didn't know that the water heater was something *we* were responsible to *turn on* – slightly different hotel room than one found in America). We hit the sack and I slept like a ROCK, as it was the first night since leaving Auburn that I slept all night long (oh good Lord, I had officially flipped to Nepal-time).

Chapter 6

Wednesday, January 19, 2011

Up like I had been shot out of a cannon, when Linda and I realized that we had forgotten to leave a wake up call. O.M.G., only work Day #2 and we were gonna be late for the bus?!?! We were buzzing around the hotel room like a couple of college kids that had overslept on their first day of class, but we still ended up getting downstairs and to the breakfast table at the same time everybody else did (whew). We all enjoyed another good breakfast, and still had time to get in several games of Steve's carried-here-from-America Bananagrams before going outside to the curbside in front of the hotel to wait for Dependra and his bus (the Bananagrams game had become slightly addictive to our entire team!). It was always entertaining just standing outside and watching the nuts-o traffic going by the street in front of the Ratna, horns honking, loose animals, etc., as we were usually in shock of the items passing by, while trying to capture the chaos on our cameras. That morning we saw an ambulance go past, so we took a picture for Julie Shoemaker and Bruce Coney, our PLH EMS friends, to tell them they might have a future here if they ever came to Nepal! Dependra and the bus arrived, and today Milan had his friend Sunneal riding along. We made a couple of stops on the way to the worksite to pick up some new handsaws, some tangerines, and a 10-gallon plastic container of purified water for the ladies to use while preparing lunch. While we were on the bus waiting for Rajesh to come back with the water, Doc proceeded to twiddle his thumbs, and when Dependra saw that, he asked if that was yoga. Doc told him no, that was twiddling your thumbs, and you did it to kill time. We all laughed. Doc rode up front in the shotgun seat to videotape the entire trip to the worksite, and he yelled back to tell the rest of us about a truck carrying propane with the sign that he just saw that said "haighly inflammable" (yes, incorrect spelling, and incorrect word –haha). I still struggled to describe this ride each day, so I think that Doc taping the whole trip would be a real adventure to watch if you weren't nauseated from the camera jerking up and down every 1.8 split seconds with the little-or-no shock absorbers on this unit. I cracked up when I saw two burros that morning, standing right in the middle of the street eating, with traffic buzzing right around them, and they didn't seem to be bothered. The trash along the streets in some of the abandoned lots was immense and beyond comprehension, and I rode along in the bus staring out the window, reflecting on how much my life was different from those that I was seeing along these journeys to and from the worksite. Like Bill said earlier, the only difference between us Americans and these people in Nepal was that our parents and other generations before us just happened to have been born in a different country, and therefore we now have the life that we do. He was so right, and when I saw some of these people, I wondered how their life would ever improve or what would ever enable them to change their current situation. But then I thought of Amala and Bagabati and their children, and how hard they and their husbands had worked to save to build their new homes to try to make changes for their own families. No wonder Amala walked by her under-construction house and lovingly stroked her new bamboo walls. Every once in a while she would catch a glimpse of me staring at her, and she always gave me this appreciative smile that made me get tears in my eyes every time. *My family tree was only different because of the place that it was planted.* Amala loved her children, her family and her neighborhood just like I loved mine, and even though I had only met her yesterday, I already saw that kinship between us. And when they all would eventually live in a new house with window openings and two doorways, and with a roof over their heads that would never leak, what a change it would make in their lives. I also couldn't help but notice that the people we passed in town, on the way to the village, all seemed to have a purpose too. They were all moving, heading somewhere; rarely did I see anybody just sitting around. They all had a reason to function, and like Doc said, they had to do something in order to earn food to eat. Unlike our country where we have food stamps and welfare, these people needed to work to survive, no matter what kind of work it was. I learned during these days that wealth and/or security there was different than wealth in my country. Wealth in the village was the security of a place to sleep at night, maybe a cow or two, some goats or chickens, maybe a shirt and a pair of pants (Dashrath had on the same clothes for many days during our visit), etc. I saw an elderly lady sitting by the side of the road that morning, and when I saw a dog step around her, I happened to think that my spoiled dogs probably had a cleaner, healthier life than some of the people that I passed each day on these streets. I saw children playing ping pong and badminton, running and playing, riding bikes, laughing, sweeping dirt, feeding cows, walking goats, and they were ALWAYS SMILING. I quickly learned the way to Amala's house on the daily bus route through the boroughs of Biratnagar, across the river by the local prison where people were washing their laundry. Out into the countryside the fields were sectioned off by raised mounds of dirt, which at this time of the year were filled with winter wheat, making them look like a patchwork quilt with varying shades of green in each square. We arrived at the worksite safely, and had another really fun day of helping these two families. That was only our second day there, and yet it seemed like the crowd of local villagers and worksite spectators continually grew larger by the hour. Several of them sat down and stayed for quite a while, helping us split bamboo. I began to recognize one man in the crowd, as yesterday he stood and watched us for a long time while holding what appeared to be his maybe-two-year old daughter. I was intrigued when I saw him come to the worksite alone this second day and he stood and watched for quite a while. I had laid down my splitting knife and walked away to go get my camera to take a picture of our team and when I returned, he was sitting on my work stool as if he had taken over for me during my break so as to not stop progress on the homes. He jumped up when I returned, to offer to give me my spot back, and I smiled as if to thank him for helping. I grabbed another knife and sat down beside of him, and he continued to work right along with the rest of us. Later that morning someone showed up with his daughter, and she ran to him, and then I kind of motioned to ask for permission to take their picture, and he was proud to let me snap a shot of the two of them together. What an adorable picture. Not only was it a thrill for me to capture their faces in my lens, but even a greater thrill to then turn the camera around and let them see themselves on the screen of my digital camera, to which they would smile and glow in delight (I so badly wished that I could understand their language to comprehend their voiced expressions). When we stopped working and walked to the lunch site around 1:00pm, I was so tickled to see that same dog, our "Mabel", *waiting for us* at the lunch tables. Her tail slowly wagged when she saw me approaching, and I said, "Nice to see you today, Mabel", and I almost saw a little smile in her eyes. She came even closer today, and after eating some of our lunch leftovers, she proceeded to lay down right outside of the lunch pavilion, as if she were our team dog (in the coming days, Linda and I would start bringing our leftover breakfast scraps with us to give to Mabel each day). Jemima did another superb job of fixing us lunch, and we definitely never went hungry on these lunch breaks (although I have to admit I was a tad picky at unusual-looking dishes and I wasn't really good at sampling everything, so the things that I did like, I filled up on). We all walked back to the worksite, and as the sun peeked out and the afternoon warmed right up, the fair-skinned Indiana red-head had to get in her backpack and get out some sunscreen! I was getting pretty darn good at whittling away at the bamboo, and it was fun watching the houses slowly start to take shape as our team was now quickly weaving the walls with the bamboo that we were then proficiently trimming. One of the local villagers that had sat down beside us to trim the bamboo started singing, and with Dependra's help we asked them if they had a national anthem, and they said yes. Rajesh talked them into singing it together, which was so cool. When they were finished singing, we sang our American National Anthem for them. Wow. About the time that school let out for the day, and the throng of school-age children along with their younger siblings came by the worksite to check out our progress, Steve got out one of his magic tricks. To the pure amusement of the crowd, he thrilled them with the "hide the blue scarf and make it reappear in my pocket trick". It was better than a Houdini Vegas act, the villagers went nuts and everybody clapped and cheered for him. I had to admit I could NEVER FIGURE OUT how he performed that trick (!), so Steve promised me that if I didn't have it figured out by the end of the build, that he would show me the guarded secret. While walking over to grab my camera out of my backpack, I heard voices behind me, and turned around, and there stood Dashrath and several of his friends. They were all lined up with their fists all extended, as if they wanted me to do the knuckle bump. Choked me up to see that. So I gave them a knuckle bump one by one down the row, and they all laughed. The pit behind Amala's house was now over four feet deep below ground level as the dirt was hauled from the pits to the house frame foundations, pan by pan atop heads. This afternoon I watched three school-age children picking lice from each other's heads, and then the rest of the day I kept imagining my head itched! Before long Rajesh was telling us to pack it in for the day, so we put all of our tools back in the HFH box and headed towards

Dependra's bus. It was always fun to turn around and glance back at the end of each day, to see the progress of the houses – the house walls were really starting to take shape! We took off for town, and as usual, the ride home was the regular anything-could-happen-at-any-moment show. First off, Rajesh cracked me up when I got into my backpack and pulled out a package of red strawberry licorice that I had brought with me from home (a gift from my sister Becky, for the trip), and I gave him his second piece of licorice (he loved it). I asked him if he had a word in his language to translate to "licorice", and he said no, but the texture reminded him of beef jerky. So then he began to call licorice "sweet jerky". He was always a hoot. We had to stop along the road at the grain weighing station where we always made a sharp 90-degree turn. On this particular day they were filling up huge bags of grain, and had them stacked upright to line the edge of the road. While we waited as they were moving the bags to let our bus pass by, Bill humorously yelled from the back of the bus, "We're gonna be sacked in!" In my opinion, Bill, Steve, and Phil all missed their calling in life by not becoming stand-up comedians with their humor and wit. It was fun to watch them when they were together and see how valuable that 50-year friendship was, and it made me stop and wonder about the length of my oldest friendships. While heading back towards the hotel, it was weird when we passed a CAR (very rare sight), and everybody looked at each other and said, "It's a *car*", at which point I was sure we were all going to have major culture shock when we returned home. We had left the worksite early today to get past the market because they had a weekly gathering there (and Rajesh knew we would get stuck in the market traffic jam if we waited until 5:00pm to leave the build site). So once we arrived at the Ratna, we had an extra hour to relax, take a hot shower, work on the journal, etc. That night at dinner, our team started talking about their memorable moments from the day, and Deb mentioned that she was looking in the window of Amala's house, and she caught a glimpse of Amala, looking around at the progress being made on her home, with a real peaceful smile on her face. She also mentioned how neat it was when she saw the look on everybody's faces while Steve was doing his magic trick, and the one kid laughed and smacked his head in disbelief. Steve added that he enjoyed watching one child's face change from fear to fun when she caught onto the trick. Doc's most memorable moment was when Amala put slats in the wall, and she wasn't measuring them and wasn't paying attention to whether they were too long or too short, and she had them all turned the same way instead of weaving them in and out of the wall. He said all he could think about was "How are we going to get this changed without her knowing it??" Larry said he really enjoyed watching two of the older village bystanders in his crowd discover the two-foot level that he had brought along in the tool box, and they were looking at it and trying to figure out what the bubbles were for. They kept playing with it and finally put it down, so Larry went over and showed them the horizontal and vertical way that a level works and explained how the tool operates (good thing Larry was a proud graduate of the Mime 101 class also). Rajesh continued to crack us up when he would announce in his sing-songy "Da plane" voice… ***"Breaking news!"*** to get our attention before he made a newsworthy announcement (wondered if he had obtained copyright usage from CNN for that??). He would always say that, whether it was to tell us all about something that had occurred that day, or forewarn us of the next day's planned happenings. We all played a few quick games of Bananagrams before turning in for the night, and then shuffled away to our hotel rooms. After climbing the flights of nasty red carpet back to our room, as Linda and I walked in the room and closed the door behind us, a MOUSE ran out from underneath my bed, went flying across the floor, squeezed under the closed door, and ran into the hallway! Major O.M.G.! YUCK, I about crapped my pants. I HATE MICE. Felix and Marilyn stopped by our room, and we chatted about the day, and I told them about the M-O-U-S-E. Then I shared with them about Dependra asking me today in his broken English about whether our team was "together?" and I told him yes, we were all together, and he said something to the effect of... "No, together, like John and Deb, and those two of them" (i.e. Larry and Cheryl), and he said, "Who are you together with?" (meaning: did I have a husband here?). So I told him no, that I was single, and then when I read the look on his face, I realized I should have lied through my teeth on that one, because that opened up the whole next set of questions in staggered English, like was I engaged, did I have children, where did my children live, etc., so I quickly steered off that path and changed the subject. So I then said to Marilyn, Felix and Linda, "What in the heck was I thinking, I should have lied and said I was married!" Then I told them that I could only imagine what a come-on line to Dependra would be... "Hey baby, how would you like me to ride on your bus and bang on your door?" I thought the three of them were gonna fall on the floor laughing, and then I apologized and said I probably shouldn't have said that, as I was sure Dependra was married and he didn't mean anything harmful by his line of questioning, and then I couldn't quit laughing myself. YUCK. A mouse had been in our room, and I then found mouse poop near my open trail mix bag, which was quickly thrown directly into the trash. O.M.G. We finally unwound and got changed into our jammies, and I caught up on the journal and reflected on Day #2. I had only been with my new HFH buds for a few days now and yet I already had huge amounts of respect for every person on our team. I could now understand why they were enthralled with doing these international HFH trips, the bond that they had built from past trips and the non-stop humor that continually flowed between all of us was addicting. The act of giving back like this seemed to seep into your bloodstream and you wanted to continue to take every trip possible to help as many people as you could in the world. I had so much fun with Amala and her family already, watching them, seeing the looks on their faces when something funny happened, or how they saw themselves on the digital screen of my camera, or how Amala looked when she was glancing at her soon-to-be house and the pride she seemed to exude. She and Bagabati had both worked hard to be able to make these changes in their lives, and it had been a joy being a part of this so far. That is, if I was not EATEN BY A MOUSE within the next 10 days. YUCK. Welcome to Nepal, land of rice and mice!

Chapter 7

Thursday, January 20, 2011

I woke up around 5:00am, and heard the first early morning Hindu chanting off in the distance. Funny to think about that, there I was at 5:00am, on the toilet peeing, in Nepal, listening to Hindu chanting. Not sure I would ever experience that again in my lifetime. Our team had breakfast, we got on the bus, and this morning I had brought Doc's little laptop along with us. It was always amazing to see the stuff we would pass each day on the way to the worksite, and instead of journaling it all down and typing it later, I just decided to capture it as I saw it. We stopped and picked up a bag of fresh tangerines at a local fruit shop, which had become the favorite fruit of our daily breaks on the worksite, and then proceeded on through the chaos. That morning we saw so much stuff, NON-STOP for 45 minutes, a shop with wedding dresses, a dog and her pup following an old man right down the middle of the street, motorcycles, rickshaws, fruit stands with hanging bananas and tangerines, a prayer house with people sitting on the floor in yoga style, where they would walk in, ring a bell and sit and pray (with their shoes left at the door), just saw a Western Union office, Larry and Cheryl saw a motorcycle where, on the back of the front wheel mudflap, they had painted a practically naked girl that only the driver could see when he looked down or turned the wheel. Dependra said we were on a street with jewelry shops, so that's why it looked like so many of the storefronts weren't open yet (the

Biratnagar jewelers must have been late-risers, and then I wondered, who could afford expensive jewelry here anyway?). Dooga was the new bus assistant riding along with Milan that particular day, and he had to step up to the plate and become the "door banger" right out of the shoot when Milan scraped up his palms when he fell trying to catch up with the bus when he had jumped off at the tangerine stop. It was hilarious watching everybody try to show Milan (Mime 101) how to rub in the hand sterilizing cleaner and we could see that it was burning his scrapes by the grimace on his face. Simultaneously, everyone on the bus began to use hand and body language, acting out how to blow on it, blow on it, rub it in, etc. It was funny to see us all looking like idiots. Seemed like we were passing so many people heading into town that morning, it was like moving upstream against a continual ant brigade on bicycles, one after another, all men riding to work in the city. We passed a flat wagon being pulled by two oxen (with the pull rope running clear through their nostrils), covered high with stacks of grain bags. I loved the little rickshaws with signs that read "School Van" on the back of them and they would be packed with kids heading to school. It always brought a smile to my face whenever I heard Rajesh call Felix, "Mr. Mexico". "Yahahaha." Rajesh had the most interesting laugh, and I was never sure if I got a bigger bang out of hearing Rajesh laugh, or watching Bill's facial reaction to Rajesh laughing. Rajesh would get so tickled with himself, to the point where you'd start laughing with him even if you didn't know what was funny. I reflected back to last night after supper when Rajesh was trying to read us the invitation to a wedding that our team had been invited to attend the next week (Larry and Cheryl had become acquainted with the future groom on their flight to Kathmandu), and Rajesh was laughing so hard that he could barely continue to read out loud (which then caused me to share with him the explanation of "after dinner sillies" in our country). I snapped back to the reality of the morning transit to overhear Doc trying to explain to Rajesh that the oncoming bicycle traffic looked like the Tour de France, and Rajesh got a big bang out of that. I am starting to recognize the route to our village, by the same small homes and living areas in the communities along the way, but none of the places we passed by would be as nice as "our homes" when they were finished (we had quickly taken ownership of the construction after Day #1). As I was riding along that morning, I also recalled how good it was to read email from home last night. It was odd how removed I already felt from my everyday life, and during the bus trip that morning, several of us mentioned that we had noticed we had left the hotel heading to the worksite with less and less each day. We had realized that, just like our partner families, we didn't need as much to survive on, as we had in our western lifestyles. Some of us were beginning to wear the same clothes two days in a row like our worksite families, and as long as we had somewhat mud-free-clean bodies (OK, some days that was questionable?), and left the Ratna each morning with our passports, our cameras, and enough clothing to stay warm for the day, we were pretty darn sufficient. On those chilly mornings, we would frequently see small fires built, with everyone squatting around them, warming their hands. They would use any trash along the road to keep the fire going. In fact at one point, when we slowed down to make a turn, I looked out the bus window and saw an elderly village lady lean over to pick up a bird feather, and throw it onto the fire. I had never been around people who recycled so much of everything in the world around them, and it made the recycling bin in my garage at home look pretty pathetic. Everyone seemed to have something to sell, whether it was tire tubes or stuffing for blankets, or hardware items, fruit, dead chickens, or a million other storefronts with everything from dried fish for soup to nuts, literally. I saw countless sets of scales, made out of bamboo platforms hung by rope, with pre-determined weights on one side. They would place whatever they were selling onto the other side of the bamboo-hung-scale until it was juxtaposed. Even in this culture, they had figured out what comprised a good deal and whether there was a profit to be made, and I began to sense that even in the poorest countries, commerce was understood. Day #3 on the worksite was very successful, as we continued to trim the bamboo and weave walls in the two houses. That morning I noticed what appeared to be a red rag tied up onto one of the bamboo beams on each house, and through the translator, Bagabati explained that their homes had been blessed the evening before by one of the local elders. Deb and I traded spots with Phil that morning and became weavers in Bagabati's house, and we quickly realized that when you were weaving, you used a whole different set of body muscles than you used when you were trimming the bamboo. But I liked this busier job, and with my busy-bee-DNA and a little training from Larry and Cheryl, Deb and I were both completing sections pretty quickly. Bagabati seemed even friendlier today; she was smiling and laughing with us, and even had her sister (another sister besides Amala) come over and motioned to me as if to ask if I could take their picture together. I think she was beginning to trust us more and more and seemed to be so thankful we were there to help them. Today when Cheryl accidentally cut her finger on a straight saw while taking Larry's place for a moment, I saw Bagabati walk over to Cheryl and put her hand on the saw, and shake her head back and forth, as if to say "no", that she wasn't going to allow Cheryl to saw any more. I loved that she was being a protective mother hen in her home's construction. Bagabati was always around working and watching us, and was so proud of her home being built. Today it was very heartwarming to see the look on Amala's children's faces when I called them each by name, and Bagabati is the same way. This morning a 12-year old boy from the village stood for a long time watching Larry cut with the hack saw, and when Larry asked him if he wanted to do it, he took the saw from Larry and became a great assistant. Larry taught him how to use it and gave him some guidance, and our crew gained another member! We broke for our mid-morning snack, and we had tea, cookies, tangerines and the Nepali version of moon pies! They were great. After I had two moon pies and a tangerine, I began weaving like a wild woman, so everybody was teasing that I wasn't going to be allowed to eat two moon pies in one break any more. Before we knew it, 1:00pm had rolled around, and we walked over to the pavilion for another great lunch. That Jemima could really cook! Mabel, who was now definitely ranking as my #1 favorite-neighborhood-stray, was back again today and whenever I talked to her, her tail would just wag like crazy. It was evident that she never got much attention in this world. She always became a very happy camper whenever I would remove the leftover breakfast items out of my backpack prior to lunch, or when I gave her some of my scraps after lunch (although she never ate the tofu and was picky about the vegetables!). I could have taken her home in a heartbeat, and I wondered what she would look like after we got her back to being a healthy dog. I took a close-up picture of her after lunch that day so I could show this Mabel to my dog-loving daughter Abby (I already knew, then and there, that this dang stray dog was just turning my heart into mush – insert heart pang here). Today there were children wading in the pond near our lunch site, catching what seemed to be minnow-size fish and putting them in small bags. Everywhere I went, I was always drawn to the small goats, as they were just so darn cute (every day in this village was like being in the petting section of the Fort Wayne Children's Zoo!). The afternoon flew by, with more "sidewalk engineers" (i.e. local bystanders sans sidewalks) coming to inspect our project. It was funny, whenever Deb or I would complete a section of woven bamboo, we would stand back, like Carol Merrill on "Let's Make a Deal" when she would wave her hands and arms in front of Door 1, Door 2 or Door 3, as if to say, "Wahlaaaa". We left the worksite, happy campers as usual, and on the way back to the hotel we stopped at a "local market" which was our version of a big flea market out in the middle of an open field, with blankets and local goods spread out all over. I really enjoyed taking pictures there, the colors of their clothing and the spices and goods they were selling were like a rainbow in my camera lens. The people were amazing. They were bartering everything, from spices and peppers to a hair cut to a face shave, to those darn little fish I just saw those kids catching today!, to cloth, jewelry, potatoes, cauliflower, squash, and other fresh vegetables of a gazillion shapes and sizes, some varieties of vegetables I had never seen before. I saw goats being butchered *on the spot,* and other bloody disgusting things that I couldn't tell what animal they were once a part of, and my desire to eat meat for the remainder of this trip came to a screeching halt at that moment. It seemed like we had turned that local market into mayhem, as the "artists" were watched throughout our entire short visit (I'm sure it was a smaller version of what a Hollywood celebrity feels when attempting to go into a McDonald's to get a cheeseburger). We took the bumpier way home and back into town, and it was always interesting to see how vehicles played "king of the mountain" on those small narrow bridges when they were coming down the road straight towards each other. The smells on the way back into town that night were almost too much, so much Nepali food/smog/vehicle exhaust, etc., that I was nauseated. My earlier career in the automotive world made me realize that the E.P.A. can be a pain sometimes, but at least in our country we had some sort of system in place to keep the air pollution under control. As Steve said tonight, we truly hadn't seen the bright "California sun" yet, it was always overcast there from the pollution. When we got home from the village, Linda and I met Phil, Steve and Bill up in the bar within the Ratna (which sat on the second floor above the kitchen), and had some laughs over popcorn and beer. Felix showed up late, and had some popcorn too. The more we hung around with those three lifelong buds, the more I wished I lived closer to them so that we could chat over dinner on occasion. Our team had fun at the evening banquet spread as usual, and then we played Bananagrams afterwards (shock!). Rajesh sensed it was starting to get late, and he proceeded to try to tell us which round was going to be the semi-final Bananagrams game for the night. It then became humorous when we all began to tease him about not being in charge of us anymore for the day. Deb piped up with, "We're not on the bus any more, so you're not the boss of me," and Bill chimed in and said, "And don't let the door hit ya in the ass on your way out." I thought we were all gonna fall off of our chairs laughing. It was great, and Rajesh laughed too and took it in the spirit of our after-dinner silliness. I headed back up to our room, caught up on the journal, and hit the hay. It was a very long day and I was whipped. It seemed like I really missed my dogs the most during the evening hours, although every time I fed my Nepali-Mabel some food scraps and I stared at her protruding rib cage and hip bones, I missed my Auburn-Mabel and her little sidekick, Flossie, even more. As I climbed into my hard-as-a-rock bed, I so wished that I could cuddle up with Floss, stick my feet under Mabel, and hear her let out that big I'm-going-to-sleep-now sigh, and we'd all be asleep in 15 seconds. I fell asleep missing them.

Chapter 8

Friday, January 21, 2011

Hard to believe it's Friday already. Last night at dinner, Cheryl gave Marilyn her watch because Marilyn's watch had broken on the worksite the day before. So, in the middle of the night when Marilyn woke up at 1:00am and looked at the watch to check the time, she didn't realize she was wearing the watch upside down on her wrist. When the watch really read 1:00am, Marilyn thought it read 6:30am. So she came down the hallway and knocked on our door for a wake up call. Linda and I heard the knock, woke up and saw that it was still dark as Hades out and sleepily debated whether to answer the door or not since it was the freakin' middle of the night. I eventually got up, jumped across the floor imagining that I was squishing night-mice as I was crossing the room, opened the door, and by that time no one was out in the hallway. I closed and re-locked the door, and we went back to sleep. At breakfast that morning (six hours later) we were all laughing when Marilyn told all of us about what had happened, and Linda and I realized it was *Marilyn* who had knocked on our room door in the middle of the night!! Breakfast was good, and Linda and I both put our food scraps into the plastic "Mabel bag" to take to our new furry friend for her lunch. It was always fun during every meal, listening to everyone's tales from their past HFH trips, and other funny stories of their lifetime. One of the things I was already thankful for was that this trip had given me a much deeper understanding that there was nothing that compared with spending several weeks away from reality, with ten other highly intelligent, humble people who cared THIS MUCH about making a difference in the world. Our possessions on the other side of the globe didn't seem to be a priority for anyone on our team. Our cars, our trucks, our homes, our cell phones, our clothes and the jewelry we left behind, the make-up we didn't wear here, or who the heck cared what your hair looked like each day. We were all focused on simply making a difference in the lives of our partner families and their community. As usual, I spent that morning typing on the Notebook on the way to the worksite, and it was again fun for me to overhear what everybody was saying and then being able to capture it as it was happening. That morning I heard Cheryl say she thought she saw someone squatting down to pull out another person's tooth with a piece of string in their mouth. I looked up from the Notebook and just saw an older man walking along the road, who possibly had stopped to squat and do his duty somewhere and then forgot to lower his front outer garment back down when he was finished, because his "Jim and the twins" were right there, hanging out for the whole world to see. O.M.G., this *was* just like National Geographic. Wow, I had to look away quickly on that one, and then I looked across the aisle at Deb and told her what I had just witnessed and that I had wanted to say, "Lower the garment, Buddy." We made one stop in the chaos of the city to buy hacksaw blades, and somebody yelled out from the back of the bus, "But do we *have* the hacksaw that the blade goes into?" and Larry answered back, "No, that will be a stop for tomorrow", and we all cracked up. As we were rounding a corner while weaving along the village road, a little girl saw our bus approaching, and she quickly scraped up the fresh dung off of the road so she could finish using it to make the dung/straw/pretzels rods (instead of having our bus run over it). Bill then eloquently added, "A little dung will do ya." Great quote! The work day went fast, and we continued to strip bamboo, weave walls and watch the houses really taking shape. One by one, our entire team took a black magic marker, and we wrote blessings and our names on a width of a strip of bamboo in a section of one of the inner walls of each of the two houses. It would eventually be covered with mud, but it was very touching to see our well-wishes and signatures in everyone's own handwriting (this is often done at HFH builds, where teams sign the wooden house beams when homes are built in other parts of the world where wood is readily available). Rajesh then translated to Amala and Bagabati that we were writing blessings and well-wishes on the walls of their homes, and they understood and seemed touched. We had duck for lunch today (I passed on that one), but I enjoyed feeding Mabel all of the leftovers we had bagged up for her from our breakfast at the hotel. Her tail was wagging like CRAZY, and today, for the very first time, she came closer, and then actually took the food right from my fingertips. Her eyes were so gentle and loving. That afternoon when we returned to the worksite, I ran around until I caught up with our favorite little black and white goat, Baaaaabbb. I picked him up, which made everybody laugh at the crazy American lady chasing their goat! It was fun scratching his nubby little antlered head, probably the first time anybody had picked up Bob, solely to scratch him, in his lifetime. Later on in the afternoon, Amala and Bagabati took us on a small tour into their current homes, and showed us how they lived. Their current homes had two rooms and a veranda, and they slept on a mud hard floor on top of a layer of loose straw, covered with blankets. They had another room that functioned as a front closet and clothes storage area, and then an attached pigeon coop. I asked Rajesh if they raised the pigeons for their eggs or did they eat them, and he answered, "Both." They cooked over a mud-molded stove, which was built above a hole in the ground where they would build a fire below, and then they had molded adobe-like formed pan holders above (I noticed that they had already made scrambled eggs in a pan for their family when we had arrived there that morning). As we got ready to pack up and leave the worksite around 4:30pm,

Deb discovered that her camera was missing. She remembered taking pictures at lunch but none in the afternoon, so on the way home, our bus stopped by the pavilion area where we routinely ate lunch each day, and Steve, Felix and Rajesh got off the bus and volunteered to go for a jog to the pavilion to see if they could find the camera there. They came jogging back empty-handed, as the camera was nowhere to be found, so everyone hoped that someone would find it and return it to us tomorrow. The ride back into town proved to be as eventful as expected, just an unbelievable sea of bodies. Bicycles, motorcycles, live animals, etc., moving towards the countryside while we were headed back into town. The following day, Saturday, would be their weekly holy day, so the men in town working in industry had gotten off early that afternoon, so we were really swimming upstream on that particular drive. I had never experienced a moving mass of humanity like that before in my life. Every night before falling asleep in the Ratna, I would replay the events of each day over and over in my mind. Those rides to and from the two houses, were replayed like live video up there in my memory bank; the faces, the sounds, the smells, the feel of the bus dodging traffic and swaying back and forth over bumpy roads, and the heavy loads of jute, sugar cane and many other agricultural crops that had been harvested slowly moving by us. BREAKING NEWS on the bus ride: Rajesh said there is a shopping area ahead in the Biratnagar commerce district and offered to let us get off and walk the few blocks to reach the hotel or just stay on the bus and they'd drive us to the hotel. So several of us jumped off of the bus at a corner, and walked maybe 10 blocks to the hotel. Wow, what an interesting world – noise, pollution, store fronts selling anything you could imagine, business fronts, medical offices, drug stores, food stands, non-stop traffic buzzing by, etc. When we arrived back at the Ratna, Linda and I had beers up in the hotel bar with the boys, and then we all had another great dinner together and shared stories from the day. After dinner we checked the Internet, and I wrote Mom a hand-written letter that I hoped to be able to mail on Sunday, if we could find a post office or someone from the hotel to mail it.

Chapter 9

Saturday, January 22, 2011
a Holy Day in Nepal

Woke up with a sore throat, but took a couple of Tylenol and was a new person. Since there wasn't going to be any work done at the worksite in observance of holy day, our group decided to take a day-trip on our "day off". Linda and I both took showers and reorganized our daypacks for some hours of relaxing sight-seeing, and we all met downstairs for breakfast at 8:00am. After everyone was done eating, Doc and Deb, Larry and Cheryl, and Phil and I met out in front of the hotel where Dependra picked us up in his bus and drove us to Rajesh's Christian church for their weekly worship service (the rest of the team spent some time at the hotel getting caught up). What a wonderful, moving experience we had at that small church. It was proof and assurance to me that even on the other side of the globe, there are others who share the same faith that I do and worship God in their hearts like I do. Many of the songs their congregation sang were familiar to me, and they were accompanied by a single guitar and a bongo drum, some songs in English and then their native language, and there were several groups of children that got up and sang for us. *"My Jesus, my Savior, Lord there is none like you, all of my days I want to praise the wonders of your mighty love. My comfort, my shelter, tower of refuge and strength, let every breath, all that I am, never cease to worship you. Shout to the Lord all the Earth let us sing, power and majesty praise to the King, mountains bow down and the seas will roar at the sound of your name."* Rajesh's wife, Anita, was in the congregation, and she had a little baby on her lap, which was the child of the guitar-player. We enjoyed watching the children and I found out that Nedia is the English-translated name of the lady I was calling PooPoo (Jemima's sister). They called the Americans up to the front of the small 18'x18' sanctuary (which appeared to have been the living room in this once-house-turned-into-church), and one by one, they draped a silk cloth around our necks and pinned a silver bow onto the scarf as a blessing and a welcome. We each had a chance to say our names and our occupation in life, as an inspiration to the children to help them to better understand who we were. The minister, Philipe, had a short sermon, which was translated in both English and Nepali. After the service, we all went outside onto the church lawn and met the rest of our HFH team (Dependra had circled back to the Ratna and brought them there so we could leave from the church to start our day together). We all enjoyed a social time with the church family, with tea and cookies (we drank <u>countless</u> cups of tea on this trip and quickly learned the difference between black tea and Nepali tea!), and took pictures with the entire congregation out on the front steps of their church. Rajesh said that on most Saturday mornings they averaged 35 people for the worship service, and even some of the Hindu-faith people in the neighborhood would send their children to this Christian church. Jaimaiche. The children of the congregation were beautiful, and they were enthralled with my camera, and wanted me to take a close-up picture of them (I loved the picture I took of three girlfriends, one holding her Bible, and one that was wearing a stocking cap that read "U.S.A."). After we said our good-byes to Jemima's congregation, we left the church and headed north towards Dharan, with everybody chatting non-stop in the rickety bus. The road took us through the industrial part of Biratnagar which we had not yet seen, where there were countless factories already established and others being built. There were very crude brick structures, which on a normal work day would have had BLACK smoke streaming out of the smokestacks, but seemed to be quiet today because of it being the holy day. We crossed the east-west highway that runs from Kathmandu to India, and continued to head north thru Itahari, where Rajesh and his wife lived (they owned one mode of transportation, a small motorcycle, and the two of them rode everywhere together on it). Dharan was a growing community with many businesses and people moving there. Rajesh said that the lot of land to build a small house on would have cost the equivalent of $50,000 USD (wow). We all began to laugh because Bill was snoozing hard enough during one point on that ride that he was sleeping through the Nepali speed bumps Dependra was flying over, which was causing the bus to practically disintegrate. Everybody then began to tease Doc, asking what kind of drugs he had given Bill that would allow him to sleep like that?!?! We passed some fish hatcheries, and came to an area where you could pull off the road and get beer and snacks, the U.S. version of the outdoor food court! We went by a cemetery, and then a huge monkey ran across the road right in front of our bus, and Rajesh screamed, "Monkey on the road! Monkey on the road!" His enthusiasm and love for life just cracked me up, and most of the time I had a hard time not laughing out loud with him when I heard his laughter. We stopped at a hardware store to buy some new "khukuri", the knives that we used to finish the bamboo at the worksite. The rest of us got off of the bus while the guys were knife-shopping, and we walked along the local storefronts and looked at the shops. I found a fabric shop and bought some material for Catherine Wilcox (General Counsel at Parkview Health) for 200 rps (approximately $3 USD), as she collects different types of fabrics from around the world. We ate lunch in a very good restaurant, Cinderella's Bakery Café, which had English signage out front, so it stood out to us among the other storefronts. Marilyn went in and ordered buffet style for all of us. We had chicken and vegetable mo-mo, chicken pizza, mushroom pizza, a curry dish with cauliflower and potatoes, and a thin chow mein salad dish. And best of all, they had soda in cans to pour over REAL PURIFIED ICE CUBES in glasses… it was beyond fantastic to have a really c-o-l-d COKE, hallelujah. After the main course, we all had fun going up to the dessert counter to pick out a dessert of our choosing. As weird as it seemed, we were all really disappointed by the dessert, as they didn't seem to use a lot of sugar in anything here, so the dessert that looked so chocolaty and yummy ended up sort of tasting like brown cardboard. I'm thinking the sign should have read, "Cinderella's Sugarless Bakery Café". We were all like a bunch of fat cats because most of the food was wonderful (pre-dessert period), and then we took turns using the one-head squat bathroom with a sign that read, *"Our aim is to keep this bathroom clean. Gentlemen, your aim will help! Stand closer! It's shorter than you think! Ladies, please remain seated during the entire performance."* On the way to Jhaba to visit a tea farm, we passed by one of the largest university hospitals in the district which was also a medical school and had a huge sprawling campus. We continued on towards Jhaba, and we drove by hundreds of burial plots and grave monuments in the woods along the road, where it looked like you could stop and bury your loved one anywhere at your choosing and then erect a monument. Wow. Then we passed a car that had just gone off the road and rolled over, with the passengers sitting out in front of it, and Rajesh announced, "Ooooh! Ooooh! Car gone mad!" It was about a 90-minute ride to the tea farm, and (up until later this afternoon) Dependra was a very conscientious driver and tried to do a good job of not running everybody off the road during the chaos. When we would pass by people along the side of the road taking a whiz, Rajesh would say, "Pee-pee break." I was amazed at how people washed their laundry by hand along a stream (and I never saw a lot of soap suds), and then they laid them out to dry over bushes (or over the dung pretzel rods!), right along the road where the dust flew non-stop. You would have thought that their clothes would all end up looking like Pig Pen in the Charlie Brown comic strip with a dust cloud behind when they walked! (Side note: Made me snicker to myself because I realized again that we were continuing to live more and more like Amala every day, when last night I rinsed out my underwear with body soap, and hung them on the coat tree in our room. I got this brilliant idea from my roomie Linda, who had previously done this instead of having some guy handling our underwear while cleaning them in the hotel laundry service. But at night when I got up to go to the restroom, I saw that freakin' shadowy coat tree and it scared the behjeeesus out of me because I thought somebody was standing there and I jumped real big.) Everywhere we drove en route to the tea farm, there seemed to be a lot of redneck bamboo scaffolding in front of buildings, with construction in progress. I asked Rajesh if their economy was prospering right now, and he said no, that actually there was a lot of unemployment. He also added that there were a lot of men working away from this part of Nepal and they were in the United Kingdom as a part of the British Army or in Hong Kong or India also (i.e. that plane packed with men we saw flying back from India). Those transit workers would send their money back home and people were beginning to build with it. It made my heart jump into my throat when Rajesh told me very matter-of-factly that he and his wife had a miscarriage a week ago, that she was about three months along when they had lost the baby. My mind immediately flashed back to her holding that baby during the church service earlier that morning, for the guitar player while she played for the congregation. He said they knew that God had a plan for them, and that there was a healthy baby in their future. I told him to tell Anita that I was praying for her, and that I had faith in their future. The bus was a funny mixture of all of us, I was typing on the Notebook, some were sleeping, Deb was reading her Nook, and of course just looking out the windows at everything we were zooming by was pure entertainment itself. Even though it was basically the exact chaos that we had been seeing for the past week, we would turn a corner, and there was something new that we had never seen before! We drove for 90 minutes in solid metropolis, the cities and towns and all levels of poverty ran together. We would pass a three-story somewhat modern-looking building, and then right next door there would be a man tending his goats. Rajesh said there were 75 districts within Nepal, (we built the houses in the Morang district) and now we were headed into the Jhapa district. Our destination for the afternoon was the Himalaya Tea Garden Factory farm. The tea was grown year-round in rows of tea plants for as far as you could see, but it was plucked March–December so the plantation wasn't really functioning while we were there. We walked the grounds, and then eventually met the manager who told us that a tea plant grows to be about 70 years old. After being harvested during those ten months, the tea was then shipped to Kathmandu or India. I was surprised that the tea leaf itself didn't have an odor, but the plantation grounds were serene and peaceful. Larry threw the factory manager a curve ball when he asked how many tea leaves were in a tea bag, which kind of stumped him, but we finally got the answer of 2.5 ounces (so how many tea leaves was that, Bananagrams-inquiring minds want to know???). Since we were there during the off-months when the factory was closed, they showed us the area where the tea leaves were laid out to dry with big fans that circulated air. We took a quick bathroom break, and I realized what a treat it was to open the bathroom door and find the pleasantry of a simple (western) toilet that had a seat/ring on it. BONUS! All along our way back to Biratnagar, people were attempting to flag down our bus not realizing it was being rented by us for the day, and so Milan sat up front and waved at them as we flew by them as if to say, "This bus is full, catch the next one" (thank goodness; at least when we drove this fast, Milan would refrain from hanging out the bus door like he did during our city-street adventures).

I took some breath mints out of my daypack and circulated them around the bus, which made me giggle. It was funny, because whenever I would pass around licorice or mints on the bus, and we would share them with Rajesh, Milan or Dependra, we would also have to mimic to them whether to suck or chew, whatever was applicable, because odds were they hadn't experienced that kind of snack before. Dusk was coming quickly, and Dependra seemed to have "the pedal to the metal" to get back to town. I could only imagine how tricky it was going to become, to dodge all of the traffic on this road once it turned dark, considering about 95% of the conveyances coming in our direction did not have headlights. During this ride on a road where we were going probably 55 mph, at one point we had to slam on the brakes because cattle were crossing the road. That would have been almost unimaginable in our culture, and yet here, cows and water buffalo were everywhere. The pace of the vehicles on the roadway during this part of the journey back towards Biratnagar seemed to have picked up and was almost at chaos stage; in fact at one point Dependra seemed to have a case of road rage with a bus that was right on our tail and honking non-stop to try to get around. Marilyn went to the front of the bus and told Rajesh to tell Dependra to start driving slower because she wanted to get her people home safely (as Steve then so eloquently put it, "Our odds of surviving this trip increase with each day that we <u>don't</u> have R&R."). Ha-ha. I proceeded to relax my head on the back on the seat and stare out the window at everything going by, and for some reason I had a flashback to Miss Barbara Brandon's kindergarten class, when we took thick oil paints in a variety of colors and put globs of paint on a sheet of white paper, and stirred them around with popsicle sticks, swirling all of the colors together. That was what it looked like out my window during that ride; the colors/people/vehicles/buildings/animals all blended and the hues in the window were swirling together. I didn't understand how people had the money to exist there, or how a child survived to adulthood. We stopped in Itahari at the nicest shopping mall around which was six stories high and had everything from soup to nuts (again, literally). I found some vacuumed sealed packages of spicy fish to take back to my son Alex, for a humorous gift for his birthday, and to Rick as an office gag gift (nothing says "I have so much respect for you" more than a package of dead fish!). Our group had so much fun just checking out all of the unusual food items on their grocery shelves, and I also picked up two boxes of Nepali tea for my parents, and headed to the checkout line. My receipt from the Gorakha Department Stores, which was an electronic printed receipt, made me smile when I looked at it and it read, "2 Ready Fish, 1 Health Tea, 1 Memory Tea". What a bargain. Almost like a MasterCard commercial: *Two gross-looking packages of dead sealed fish with buggy eyes, + two boxes of tea = 376 Nepali rupees (equivalent of a little over $5 USD). Foreign tourists experiencing an awakening to human conditions in the Third World = priceless.* The next 30 minutes were a pure crapshoot ride back into Biratnagar, as the headlights on our bus looked like they should have been replaced two years ago, and the majority of the traffic coming towards us did not have any headlights whatsoever. I kept smiling to myself because no matter how many people I would ever share this story with, there were only 14 other people in the entire world who would ever understand exactly what I was talking about at that moment in time. I was amazed that we hadn't witnessed any serious injuries up to this point on the roadways on this trip, as there were people on bicycles, riding on this road where everybody was flying like a bat out of hell, and the only light illuminating their path was the two-candle brightness of the lights *from the buses whizzing by them.* It was NUTS. It was then 7:30pm Saturday there on the bus, which would have made it around 6:30am Saturday morning back home in Auburn. I wondered if Abner was working at her bank that morning, and if Alex, Ashley, Baylie and Gage were awake, in a different time zone on the other side of the world. I thought about yesterday being Alex's

82

birthday and that it had been weird not being able to talk to him or do something to celebrate his 29th birthday (wow, how could my son be that old already?). I love my family oh so much. Through a divine act of God, we somehow arrived safely back at the hotel just in time for dinner, and proceeded to play several games of Bananagrams after dinner, with Deb being the grand champion two nights in a row. Man, she could come up with incredible words! We started singing commercial jingles, "Oh I'd love to be an Oscar Mayer weiner, that is what I truly want to be, for if I were an Oscar Mayer weiner, everyone would be in love with me." Then we were all driven nuts by the fact that we couldn't remember the Oscar Mayer bologna song, and finally it came to me and we all started singing out loud, "My bologna has a first name, it's O-s-c-a-r. My bologna has a second name, it's M-a-y-e-r. I love to eat it every day and if you ask me why I'll say, 'Cause Oscar Mayer has a way with b-o-l-o-g-n-a.' " It was a hoot! Went back to our rooms, and Linda and I fell asleep while talking like two kids at 4-H camp in bunk beds. We would often talk about our families each night before falling asleep. Linda told me stories about her husband, their daughter and pets (including an adopted German shorthaired pointer, and a horse!), and we were laughing when I told Linda how we had recently found out that my Auburn-Mabel had wonderful hidden hunting talents after her first bird dog training adventure with Alex. We also laughed because we got silly and started imitating Bill singing "Dung, dung, dung, dung, duunnngggggg" (to the tune of the theme song from "Dragnet", or the Tums commercial). At least there hadn't been a second mouse sighting, and we eventually fell asleep after laughing ourselves silly.

Chapter 10

Sunday, January 23, 2011

When we woke up it seemed weird that their holy day had been on a Saturday, so there we were on a Sunday, heading to the worksite?!? We got up and ate breakfast at our usual time, and then had enough time for the gang to play a quick game of Bananagrams before getting on the bus (regular version, first one finished with all of their tiles said "peel" and everybody grabbed another letter until a winner was determined). We had all decided Dependra's bus was pretty indescribable, the way it had seats for about 29 people, but half of the seats continued to break through the seat frame foundations, and the outside ones were sometimes wet during the morning rides from the dew that had leaked in through the windows overnight. The overhead compartments were covered with red/brown/cream velour leaf-print material, adorned with beads near the driver and shag skirting/fringe hanging down in the front of the bus for decoration (OK, the use of the word "decoration" might have been an exaggeration). I got the impression they had attempted to dress up the bus for the Americans by covering the seatbacks with white seat covers, and the door that Milan continually banged on was adorned in red-painted-chicken-scratch letters that spelled out, "WEL-COME". On the ceiling of the bus there was a mosaic pressed-plastic design that reminded Felix and me of an antique ceiling in an old building. I'm pretty sure the windows/floors/seats hadn't been cleaned for ages, as the day before on the trip to the tea factory, when Rajesh wanted me to come forward in the bus and sit beside him, the DUST FLEW out of the seat when he patted it as to motion to me to come sit there (no wonder the computer screen continually drew dust like a moth to a flame). Our first stop was Rajesh's church, and besides Jemima and Nedia climbing aboard, Rajesh proceeded to introduce us to the new volunteers from his church that were on the bus with us and would be joining our team for the day, Maren and Missal. We made it through Biratnagar human/animal traffic to our daily tangerine stop and passed the commerce area heading out of town to the village. I was always amazed at some of the highly stacked loads that men were pedaling on bicycle-drawn wagons. Many times I saw the cyclist walking the bike because he could no longer pedal, which meant the load had to be extremely heavy; then why in the heck didn't the bike tires pop? There had to be a real science in knowing the exact pressure in which to inflate those bike tires, pre-load and post-loading?? It was extremely foggy, but the sun seemed to be hiding behind the haze so we all hoped that it would soon warm up (seriously, I didn't know how Dependra was able to see what was heading towards us that morning). Rajesh looked around, out the bus windows, and announced in his "da plane, da plane" voice, "Breaking news, bad foggy", which had me laughing (and he has also started to call me "Kay-Kay" during our days at the worksite). We figured out that Maren's wife was the guitar player at the church service yesterday and that his daughter was the one that was in the front of the children's choir. He also shared with us that her name was Marilyn, also spelled "Meroleen" in Nepali, which made our own Marilyn smile! On the ride to the worksite I shared a bus seat during the ride with Felix, and he told me about his family in Mexico, and how his sister chose to give up her life and adopt a child and how it had changed her life. Felix said this area of Nepal reminded him a lot of "TJ" (which was how he referred to Tijuana, Mexico) and he told me about the environment that he lives in on a daily basis. He showed me pictures on his camera of the streets and the neighborhood houses where he lives. Felix felt that our team members might view Nepal as a poor area that we are just visiting on a temporary basis, but that this area is the "norm" compared to where he lives every day. This trip had already enlightened me about my own existence and what my daily life consists of, and listening to Felix talk about his life in Mexico, it hit home even further. Felix had the impression that most of the people in Nepal appeared to not have the slightest idea of our western world concept of hygiene, and yet we both agreed that we were surprised at how healthy the people that we came in contact with seemed to be. Felix said that he felt that nature had been good to them to keep them resistant to germs and had enabled them to have lived as long as they had. The children in the small villages along these one-lane, bumpy, dirt roads on the way to our build site would now frantically wave at us each day as they ran along beside our rumbling white bus. They were adorable, and they were so happy to see us pass by. We got so much done at the worksite that day; we continued to trim bamboo pieces, and many wall sections were woven on both houses all the way to the roof line. Around 11:00am we walked over to the Sree Primary School for a visit, which was the community school closest to the build site (maybe 300 yards away from Bagabati's home). The one-story school was approximately 20 years old, and was located on land that was donated by a community member. The outside of the school was painted a Kermit the Frog shade of green, with melon trim around the windows and doorways. It was a primary school, made up of 245 students, grades 1–5, but less than 30 kids were there on that particular day, as the regular school year is April thru December. Since January was considered part of their school break during the colder winter months, the children who did choose to come to school during this winter break only went to school from 10:00am–4:00pm each day, Sunday thru Friday. When school returned back in full session they would be adding another morning class in the spring, lengthening the daily school hours. Each day the school shut down for a 1:00pm break, and all of the children would leave school and run to their nearby homes in the village for lunch (you had to appreciate that close-knit community and the simple way they lived). There was the principal and two other teachers on staff during this winter break, and the principal told us that the teachers received local training, and that they were enduring a current teacher shortage. They had already made plans to expand the school into higher grade levels, as the children currently studied Nepali, English, mathematics and social studies. The children were so honored and happy that we visited, and it was easy to see that several of the girls had apparently worn the very best dress that they had to see us here today. They all sat in a semi-circle on the grass while the principal talked to our group, and they had their school books, tablets, and their pencils in front of them in piles as they sat cross-legged. There was one little boy that had the moxie to stand up and sing two solo songs, in front of the whole school and the guests. What bravery! The other children stood up and joined him in singing their national anthem, and then we sang a chorus of Amazing Grace for them. We followed the teachers on a short tour of a couple of their classrooms, and it was interesting to see everything that was displayed on their school room walls. There were brightly colored signs of the alphabet, numbers, and how to stay sanitary in their environment, (one caricature was of a man squatting and pooping, I kid you not!), etc. We gave gifts of some candy and small presents for the school to distribute, and the principal thanked all of us for coming to their community to help them. With Rajesh interpreting, the principal told us he had been watching the progress of the two houses we were working on (he witnessed the construction through the tree line that stood in between the two houses and the school), and he was proud to see the change in his community. Before we headed back to the worksite, Steve did his "blue scarf appears in my pocket trick" for all of the school children *(I still couldn't figure it out!),* and again the crowd of astonished fans went nuts.

If Steve ever got bored living along the ocean in his home in California, he could have a HUGE gig with his magic tricks in this village! Back at the worksite, we finished up another section on the houses, and then we all broke for lunch. Our beloved Mabel was back again, and as we gave her our breakfast morning leftovers from my backpack, she seemed to put her nose in the air and ignored our breakfast offerings, but quickly scarfed down the leftover pork off of my plate from lunch (is a "picky starving dog" an oxymoron??)!!! She had learned to work the food line! Haha! I loved the way her tail now wagged when I simply *looked* at her and made eye contact, so different from the untrusting dog of just a week ago. Rajesh had to be off-site for a HFH meeting back in town this afternoon, so we kind of organized ourselves and we headed back to the worksite and just continued to work unsupervised (What!?! No breaking news this afternoon?!?). The team began carrying mud for the house foundation on big, flat, disc-shaped pans on top of our heads, and it was great to watch that and get pictures of everybody (I was still working on bamboo with Doc and Phil). Deb's camera was still M.I.A., and we're still not sure if it walked away from the worksite that day, or whether she lost it at the lunch area, but either way no one had returned it. Bummer. The word spread through the village that her camera was missing, and an elder from the village came this morning and told us that he had a vision that the camera was now in the village "over in that area". She would have just been thrilled to have had the camera card returned out of it, and we all laughed that probably nobody would be able to 1) keep it charged or 2) figure out the camera functions to know how to use it. Luckily, Doc had brought along a back-up digital camera besides his expensive professional-looking camera, so Deb still had a camera she could use to capture her own pictures for the rest of our trip. Everybody worked really hard today, and we were all sore, tired and extremely dust-covered on the ride home (we were all commiserating that we had sure better have hot water in our rooms when we got back to the Ratna because we were all hoping and praying for relaxing showers tonight). I glanced over while typing and watched Deb find a wet towelette in her backpack, and wipe off her face and hands. I couldn't believe the dingy dust left behind on the suddenly brown towelette (nor could she). Nothing like a little Nepali dust and mud to help one's lungs and skin tone ☺. The smoke coming out of the smokestacks of the factories we were passing on this ride was just spewing out like crazy. Definitely no E.P.A. regulations intact here today and the pollution was horrid. We were joking that we should have put on air-filter masks prior to arriving in Kathmandu to somehow examine all of the crap that we had been inhaling into our lungs while in the cities in Nepal (the villages in the countryside didn't seem nearly as hazy/polluted). We passed by a local flea market, and as Linda so eloquently put it, "It's just a swarming mass of humanity." With each passing day and with each one of these trips to and from the village, I was certain that I had never witnessed anything like this before in my lifetime. I continued to be amazed at how all of these people lived in this community, and I wondered what they ate and how they made a living. Deb just said that Bagabati came to her today, tapped her on the shoulder, and put her hands up as if to say, "Isn't this glorious?", and then she gave Deb a "thumbs-up" sign. As we turned a corner back inside the metropolis, I swore we were inches away from the bus next to us, so I stuck my camera out the bus window and took a picture down the side of our bus, capturing the millimeter gap. I still can't believe we don't see more animals hit on the road, as they are ALL OVER THE PLACE. It wasn't uncommon to see a goat herder walking down the road, herding maybe 20 goats out in front of her. Only two of them would be tethered to her by rope, and she would give them a lengthy lead like I give Mabel and Flossie on our walks to the park. The other 18 goats would just be trotting along beside. At 55 mph, our bus would fly by the whole goat herd, inches away from them, and none of the goats would even seem to flinch. ?!?!? Deb just saw a guy riding in a rickshaw holding a goat, and we said he was taking supper home, like KFC. Deb said no, that would be KFG. Good one! The wit of my teammates was addictive. I was surprised that my mind was continuing to absorb the sights and sounds from each of these bus rides and that my brain hadn't already crashed on overload. Tonight there was a traffic policeman (adorned with uniform and whistle) who flagged us down and jumped past Milan and into the open door and onto our bus for a ride. He rode on our bus for several blocks and jumped off right before we got to our hotel (we all made a quick mental note that Milan didn't tell the police officer to get off the bus like he had others along our rides!). We were always so thankful when the bus finally screeched to a stop at our destination, coming or going, and we found ourselves still breathing and in one piece. The dinner that night was good, it was a continental meal, with pasta, Thai, and a variety of food, and fried bananas. We played Bananagrams, took hot showers, and CRASHED.

My dear family at a surprise going-away party.

Larry and Cheryl, purchasing a hand-woven rug in Kathmandu.

Felix, Marilyn (our fearless HFH team leader), and Linda.

Dashrath,
my knuckle-bump buddy.

Babita,
carrying dirt for her
home's foundation.

My beloved
Nepal Mabel.

Our blessings to the family, written on a bamboo wall of the house (before being covered with mud).

Bagabati and Deb during a break.

Our team, visiting the Christian church where Rajesh and Jemima worship.

The bi-weekly lending cooperative meeting in the village.

Rajesh (HFH Project Coordinator) and Doc Egli.

Mudding the walls of the Devi family home.

Bill, after a hard day of mudding.

The Devi family, in front of their nearly completed home (less roof peak): Babita, Anita, Amala, Dashrath, Ram, and "Grandpa".

The Singh family: Ranju, Umesh, Ramesh, Bagabati, and Rajindar.

My new friend,
Jemima, who
unselfishly gave
up her life for
11 days to be our
lunch cook at
the worksite.

The band
of brothers
with a
50-year
friendship:
Phil, Steve,
and Bill.

Our
wonderful
Himalayan
guides and
trekking
porters (and
Bananagrams
competitors!).

"Attempting" to experience the physical load the porters carried (I lasted about 20 seconds).

The Taj Mahal, in all of its splendor.

One of the treepies eating from my hand.

The wild tigress, nothing separating us but air.

(photo courtesy of John Egli)

Chapter 11

Monday, January 24, 2011

Up bright and early, as we had to leave the hotel an hour earlier than usual to get to the worksite for a community interaction with the villagers from the Jeevan Bikas lending/borrowing group. It was always fun to get downstairs to the hotel banquet room early, and watch everybody come down for breakfast and report in on what quirky things had happened during the nighttime hours on their floor of the Ratna. Phil was ecstatic that morning, because he got "Two towels!", which started out my day with laughter. Several folks were still having trouble with hot water in their rooms, or getting laundry back, or Internet connections; yes, there was always something that seemed to be comically amiss in that hotel. We had a flat meat patty this morning for breakfast, and it was funny, because when I asked Rajesh what kind of meat we were eating, he first paused and thought how he was going to answer us, and then paused again, and finally replied "chicken." Doc looked at me and smiled real big, and I had a hard time not laughing out loud. I was never quite sure whether Rajesh was telling us the truth about what we were eating, or just told us what he thought we wanted to hear (either way, you could have bet my last dollar that *my* meat patty was gonna get wrapped up and taken to Mabel in the backpack – no meat for "Kay-Kay" after viewing the butchering adventure in the flea market). Everybody on our team always had a story to tell from past adventures in their life, and we spent our time during these group meals all laughing together. We also had fried potato chips that day as a part of our morning smorgasbord, and even though I couldn't say that I had ever had potato chips for breakfast before, they were good! The ride to the worksite was eventful as usual, as we had to stop and wait for Jemima who was buying vegetables at a local market which she would eventually use to prepare our lunch. While we were stopped and waiting, a local man hopped onto the doorstep of our bus beside Milan, and Milan shook his head no and told him to get off the bus (unlike the traffic cop incident from yesterday). After the stranger departed the bus, Felix immediately hopped up from his seat near the front of the bus, and told Milan that in the future if anybody got on the rickety bus, he should switch to flight-attendant-mode, and explain the safety features of the aircraft, pointing out the overhead lighting, oxygen masks and where the emergency exits were. We were all laughing so hard as Felix then dramatically showed Milan how to do this, putting up his first two fingers on each hand and with the skill of a Broadway actor, vividly flicking his wrists while pointing from the rear to the front of the dilapidated ceiling of the bus as if to show the emergency lighting, followed by pretending that he was grabbing a dropped oxygen mask and putting it over his nose and face, etc. (in fact the memory of that just made me laugh so hard that I spit onto the computer screen as I was typing, as I could again picture Felix shaking his butt like a female flight attendant). Of course while the rest of us were laughing so hard we were practically rolling in the filthy bus aisle, Rajesh proceeded to translate what we were so amused about because Milan's eyes were darting around for understanding, as he was totally lost and clueless as to what Felix had just tried to dramatize for him. That Felix was a hoot the whole trip! Whenever the bus stopped for traffic, or for someone to jump off to buy something, it was always amazing to see what was *right outside* of the bus door. Today I watched as this lady had a whole pile of dishes sitting out along the storefront of her business, that apparently she was going to wash outside (with cold water of course), with stuck-on food still coating the dishes from the night before, or maybe from breakfast? I couldn't believe there wasn't more noticeable sickness, as you had to wonder how everything remained sterile enough to kill germs (even for us, as I assumed our lunch plates and utensils were washed in cold water when I would see them in containers near the local water pump at the lunch site). I glanced over and watched this elderly woman, sitting on a doorway stoop, and I wondered what she had been through in a lifetime of rough existence here. Her face was wrinkled and weathered, and she had a wooden cane that she walked with. Her hair was long and gray, but she smiled when I stepped out of the bus to take her picture. When I got back on the bus, Dependra was reading a local newspaper while patiently waiting for Jemima to return with the vegetables, and he told us that a bomb blew up in a church yesterday in Iraq, killing 22 people. I felt so out of touch with the rest of the world; almost every day we had asked if anybody had heard anymore about Gabby Giffords, the congresswomen who was shot before we had all left the States, but we hadn't heard any updates on her while there. Every once in a while we would be able to see news channels and hear them in English through the fuzzy reception of the hotel room TV, but we were never in the room at the right time of the day to see a global news update. It was colder that morning, and I had on two layers of long underwear shirts, then my Parkview hooded sweatshirt (with the hood up) and my Cabela's coat on top of that. We kept reminding ourselves that we were up an hour ahead of our usual departure time, so hopefully it would warm up like it did yesterday (when we had worked in short sleeves most of the day and got some more sun on our white bodies). There were small fires burning all along the route today, with everybody gathered around them for warmth. It was no wonder the air seemed so polluted from the perpetual haze that never burned off until mid-day. On the way through the city, Deb saw a lady with her daughter squatting, aiming for a crack, while the mother just stood in front of her waiting for her to "go". It was different to be in a culture where everyone relieved themselves wherever/whenever it was a necessity most of the time. There were no trash receptacles whatsoever, they all just swept their trash to the curb with a crude few pieces of long reeds (their version of our straw broom), and then a "trash truck" would come by and shovel it up. Of course they kept everything they thought they could burn, recycle, or eat in some fashion. Felix and Linda sat behind me talking that morning, and in front of me were Nedia and Jemima, yakking away in Nepali. Doc was in his usual shotgun seat up front, Deb and Cheryl were chatting over to my left, and in the back of the bus I could hear Marilyn, Steve, and the three stooges "Larry, Curly and Moe" (Larry, Phil and Bill) chatting away about farming and other things. The sun continued to rise on our drive, and it was a beautiful tangerine orange in the hazy sky. We veered to the far left of the road to avoid a wide load of sugar cane on a bridge, which made everyone grab for their cameras. The litter and waste in the fields/ditches was immense. I kept thinking that the whole trash issue was the most striking difference from the way I normally lived, as in our country we usually attempted to keep our society a little neater. Our bus passed by a tiny boy, maybe three-years old, wearing a long-sleeved hooded sweater, naked from the waist down, snot dripping from his nose while enjoying a sucker, running along and smiling at our bus. We drove past a wooded area, where a man was squatting with his butt hanging over a log, taking a dump. Rajesh said, "Breaking news", and Deb said, "No, that's breaking wind", and we all laughed. Milan's cell phone kept ringing to the "Happy Birthday" ring tone (yes, it was like we were in some freaky time warp when we would be driving along looking out the windows at this antiquated society and then hear a cell phone ring). He was not answering and the song was loud and irritating, so we joked that someone had to show him where the ignore button was on his phone. More eye-darting and no understanding. We arrived at the worksite and put down our supplies, and walked a short distance to take part in the biweekly meeting between the female borrowers in the village and the JB microfinance people. The women were the accountants in their families, and they were all sitting in this open area in front of one of the homes in the village, on this straw-covered area on the ground, cross-legged, yoga style, in their brightly colored wraps with their sandals off to the side. They sat nine rows deep, five women across in each row, and they had come to either pay money back on a loan, or give the bank representative their money to save. There were some men standing off to the side of this gathering to watch what was taking place, but it was interesting to see that the women were the ones who controlled the finances in the families within this village. In every row of women sitting before us, there was a chairman, and a secretary, and others were members of represented sections, and they explained that the women collectively elected a new leader of this JB banking group each year. We learned that Habitat was just one section of the local lending for this village, and I was in awe to witness the amount of trust it took to make this all work. *No receipts* were given for any paper money handed over, just a solo lending representative, taking money at a small table and writing everything down in ledger books *by pencil,* witnessed by a village woman sitting on a chair beside him. Rajesh started out the gathering by having each one of us introduce ourselves and say what we did in life (with him translating), as an inspiration to those attending. He asked the women of the village to share the differences that these loans had made in their lives, and some answered that they had then been able to buy land, had gotten loans for crops, or were now able to take care of their family, etc. When asked how many were saving for houses, 12 women raised their hands as being on the waiting list and currently saving money for a future home. It was cute to see Amala and Bagabati sitting in their rows, continually peeking around the women sitting in front of them to make eye contact with us, smiling. Being married was a requirement for participation within this community banking group, so all of the women sitting in front of us that morning were married. One of the group leaders asked about the United States; she wanted to know about the people, where they lived, how they lived, what they did. Larry told them it was a large country, that we had many nationalities of people in one country, and that we lived in a country which people desired to come to. He explained that our country was large enough to have many varying climates, that some of us had snow, while others had sun, that we had the same soil they did, but that we also had desert and mountains too. Rajesh translated that Larry and Cheryl's farm in Indiana was very large, and that only three people farmed it, and that Larry could do a lot with machinery. We asked Rajesh to translate to the women that we identified with them. We saw that they were hard working women, and we were the same kind of women and grandmothers that they were. We wanted them to know that we enjoyed taking pictures of their children because we missed our own families while we were with them. They all looked at us after Rajesh translated, almost as if they now understood what we women felt. They asked Larry if he had rice paddies on his farm, and Larry explained that he grew corn and soybeans. They asked about our meals and what we ate, and Rajesh translated about the normal things in our diets and the meats we ate and he even explained about our "fast food" (we were pretty sure that he left out the part about how we ate beef ☺). Rajesh translated how Doc went out behind his house in Topeka to his natural habitat area where the ice was frozen over on his pond, and he had to drill a hole in the ice so he could go fishing. Felix wanted him to translate that his community in Mexico was just like this area of Nepal. Doc also wanted Rajesh to ask the women how could they sit that long without getting stiff (cross-legged)?!?, and they laughed and replied that they sat like that for hours on end, out of habit. The banker shared that most of the women brought about 20 rps every other week and the bank paid them 8–12% interest, or a housing loan was based on a diminishing rate of interest. If someone in that group of women couldn't make their payment on any given week, then other neighbors would step up and cover for their loan, as it was a community cooperative. They explained that they had to give a dowry when their daughters got married, that gold was compulsory and usually the dowry was made up of visible things so the community would see that it was a good thing (i.e. if you gave a motor bike, then the community could physically see that). They also explained that the women there were continually fighting for more education in the community, so that they could have something else for their future. They said that even in their village, the dowry system was still in place, but people were becoming more focused on education. Most marriages were still arranged marriages, but the children remained close and didn't move far away. We thanked them for explaining this process to us, and then the meeting broke up and we walked the short distance down the village walkway, over to the worksite and began our day with more weaving and bamboo trimming. Around mid-morning we heard the sound of beating drums in the distance and Rajesh said that was a funeral procession. The somber parade of funeral attendees soon went by the homes that we were working on, with family members slowly walking by, wailing, crying, etc. It was evident that it didn't matter what culture we were in, death was still inevitable, and I felt so sad for those families who had apparently lost a loved one. That morning the sheets of aluminum roofing were hoisted up onto Amala's house and screwed into place. Wow, how amazing would it be for their family, to stand in their house during the first rain storm, and hear the rain pound against that aluminum and no longer worry about it leaking through a thatched roof? We broke for lunch, and after we ate we walked to a nearby government school, which was a short distance from our lunch area. The entire school had prepared a special presentation for us, and I couldn't believe the number of children, all in forest green sweaters, white shirts and green pants, with both girls and boys wearing knotted blue and white striped ties, spread out on the lawn for an assembly in our honor. Since this was their winter break and they considered these cold months, most of the children also had on a stocking cap or a scarf wrapped around their head, even though we were in T-shirts or simple long-sleeved shirts. There were hundreds of children staring at us, which was interesting to see so many children here, apparently since their parents paid for them to attend this school, they must have continued to attend school during this winter season, unlike the community school we had earlier visited. Each member of our team was ceremonially adorned with a marigold lei, and our foreheads dotted with red dry ink. Marilyn was called up front as the leader of our group and presented with a special cloak and head dressing. The principal gave a welcome on behalf of the school in his rather broken English…

"As the principal of this school on behalf of the whole school family, I would like to express my warm welcome to all of our honorable guests of the USA and Mexico. I would also like to extend a warm welcome to the JB guests and Habitat for Humanity guests from Nepal. Today is a very great honor for us to meet you here in Nepal, as there is a very small chance for us to ever visit your country. In the same way I am so glad to the Habitat for Humanity for the help for the homes and we're finally getting to meet the guests of the different countries and your time is very valuable that you are making for the homes. I think you are approaching to complete by tomorrow. The program should begin now and that you will all enjoy the performances."

The first choir sang a welcome song… The words were,

We welcome you with a heart full of joy,
We welcome you with a heart full of happiness.
We welcome you with our tears and sorrows,

Who knows, it may bring a different tomorrow.

We welcome you with our dad and mom,
We welcome you with our brothers and sisters.
We welcome you with our friends and chums,
Who knows, it may have to cross many humps.

We welcome you for our blissful nature,
We welcome you for our shining future.
We welcome you for our healthy survival,
Who knows, it may look for another arrival.

Wow, if that didn't get to you, I'm not sure anything ever would, as it was so touching to see those children singing their hearts out. I talked to their teacher afterwards; she told me she wrote both the words and music to that song. Incredible. I think that should be our HFH Nepal 2011 theme song. The performance area had a sound system (complete with two microphones) and was covered with colorful parachute material hanging down and flowing in the wind, shading an area approximately 25'x50'. We were seated up front on wooden chairs, and the children all sat cross-legged on the ground in a huge grassy area, with their teachers sitting at the end of each row, just like they would in our school assembly programs. The performing children were dressed in festive attire with thick eye-liner, colorful make-up, and adorned in beaded costumes of the Nepali people. They performed a dance for us, and they were so beautiful. You could tell it was a quite an honor to have Americans come and visit. The principal told me the school was made up of grades 1–8; approximately 427 children attended school there, and the principal appeared to be about the same age as my son Alex (i.e. young). The children were very well-behaved, watching us and the performances. Two little children from the nursery school class came up to perform for us, and they were so shy the teacher came up to inspire them, but they never did sing "Head and Shoulders, Knees and Toes". Two girls who looked like they were maybe fifth or sixth graders performed a slower native dance in costume, recognizing the different cities of Nepal. Then we saw a short drama presentation. One of the young actors had on a fake mustache which was hilarious, and was portraying a drunk after drinking whiskey with his friends. In the next act, his son was dying and the doctor told the father-figure that whiskey affects the whole family, and he told him to save the future of his son and quit drinking. He said that after today he would not touch a drop of whiskey. He prayed that God would forgive him and help him take care of his family. The young actors were so cute, and they did a great job! Marilyn went up front to represent us, and she spoke to the audience saying, "We wish to thank all of you for asking us to come here today, the privilege is all ours. We came here basically because we knew we could tour your country, and have the chance to work with you and learn about you like we are doing today. We really appreciate everything that you've done for us, and we might want to come back some day!" We got up and sang the American National Anthem, and then we had the chance to tour some of the classrooms (and we were pretty sure that the one young female teacher was hitting on our beloved and frisky Bill, and hey, with his suave and witty charm, who could blame her?). I took a picture of a piece of lined school paper hung on one classroom wall, printed in elementary school handwriting in all capital letters that said "WE SHOULD NOT QUARREL". Priceless. During our tour of the classrooms, I made eye contact with one of the boys that stops by our worksite each day and appears to be a friend of young Dashrath. He stepped forward, and I had someone take my camera and snap a picture of the two of us together. Made me wonder what the next 20 years of life would bring for that ten-year old boy. The principal told us after the program that the children who attended the school were from all over the district, some from 22 km away, and that enough rich people paid for their kids to attend here that they were able to take some of that money and provide scholarships for 60 other village children who would not have been able to afford that kind of an education. We left the school area, and walked the short distance back to the worksite, cutting through the sugar cane fields. In the midst of the walk and group chatter, we began laughing because Linda discovered that the plastic bag that she had been carrying all day for the team wasn't the daily afternoon team-snack-supply that she thought it was, instead it was filled with trash! When we came to the clearing where we could see the worksite, we were surprised to see how much mudding Amala had completed on her house while we were at lunch and the school assembly. She was like a mudding machine! We continued to work throughout the afternoon, and Cheryl and I enjoyed seeing that same father and daughter visiting us again today. The little girl was warming up more and more; we kept teasing her to slap our hand and give us five, so we hoped by the end of the week we would see that happen. The ride back to the hotel was exciting as usual; there was another huge flea market along the road, and I told Deb it was just like Shipshewana!

Chapter 12

Tuesday, January 25, 2011

Just when we thought this trip couldn't get any more bizarre! When we returned to the hotel last night, we had been notified that the bus drivers in the city had gone on strike. Apparently one of their drivers was sentenced to eight years in prison after hitting and killing a pedestrian, and so in protest of that decision, the drivers were now on strike. What that meant to us was that we no longer had a secure way of getting to the worksite for the final three days of work without the bus and Dependra to drive it. So after breakfast we all camped out in the hotel, used Steve's paid Internet coupon for the hotel Wi-Fi (which was supposedly a 24-hour coupon, but the group had now been using it for DAYS) and got caught up on emails, played Bananagrams, etc. Rajesh spent the morning making phone calls like a United Nations negotiator, and attempted to contact the police for an escort and secure a bus to take us to the worksite. Finally we were told by the hotel staff to be in front of the hotel in five minutes. So we gathered in the lobby, and eventually were led by a hotel representative to the local police station, which was a short walk away. Of course 11 fair-skinned people, standing out in front of a police station in Biratnagar, Nepal, brought on just a *slight* amount of attention. So as we stood and waited for what we assumed would be Rajesh and Dependra to show up with our bus, it was fun just watching everybody watching us. This was a good call on the part of Rajesh, as the police station was definitely the safest place for us to board a bus during the bus strike (if we had done that in front of our hotel, it's hard telling what kind of riot that might have caused). In the meantime, we were all in awe of the activities surrounding the police station. I noticed an old man, sitting yoga-style, on a front stoop across the street, but couldn't figure out what he was doing. So I crossed the street and found out that he was binding books with glue. Sure enough, our Dependra-driven bus soon came down the street with the Habitat for Humanity banner hung ON FRONT (as if that would release us from the community hatred of someone crossing the bus drivers' strike line). We all climbed aboard and began our course towards the countryside, *led by a two-vehicle police escort procession* (I looked at everybody and said, "I'm definitely not telling my family about this until I am home!"). The police truck in front of us must have had 15 *armed guards* on the back of it, and with all light-skinned passengers lining the window seats so the local city people could see that it was being used for a transport vehicle instead of a local bus working as usual and defying the bus strike order (so Jemima came and sat beside me on an inside aisle). We proceeded through town with everyone staring and gawking. When we reached the edge of town, the larger police vehicle pulled off to the side, and we continued to be led by a smaller police escort with two armed guards in the back of it, with lights flashing on the police vehicle. Other than following police with guns this morning (?!?!?) the ride was about the same (Deb just saw a rickshaw driver texting and driving, wished I had gotten a picture of that for some Parkview advertising for our recent "Don't Text and Drive" marketing blitz!). At one point during the ride to the worksite, Jemima looked over at me, and with tears in her eyes, she told me she was going to miss me. She said we were friends now, and that she hoped I continued to pray for their congregation once I got back home. I told her how much coming to their church service on Saturday had meant in my trip to Nepal, and that I would continue to pray for all of them. I asked her if she had access to email, and she said yes, and I told her that we could continue to communicate via Facebook. Jemima was a kind soul with warm eyes and a gentle heart, and I silently reflected on how much we were the same. She loved the same God that I did, and yet we were on the other side of the globe and worlds apart from each other. Every work day in my world, I put on a business suit and high heels, curled my hair and drove to work in my car, where my mind went 125 mph as I was simultaneously pulled in many directions assisting high-level executives in a healthcare corporate office. Jemima was the wife of a minister and an excellent cook, and she had given up two weeks of her ministry life to fix meals for us, and make us feel welcome in her country. If our roles were reversed, would I have been able to take time away from my job to welcome 11 Nepali's into our country, and would I have enabled them to feel this comfortable with me? This woman with round cheeks and short dark hair, and who stood less than five-feet tall, was an amazing, gifted, Christ-loving woman, a living symbol of service to others. We all noticed there was no truck traffic on the roads that day; it was as if time has stopped in their world with the drivers' strike and our bus was running solo. The rickshaw traffic had doubled! The police escort parted from us once we hit the dirt roads and then it was the usual ride to the worksite, among local village huts, cows and bulls, rickshaws, bicycles, people squatting and eating, children playing, goats tied up... as we would say at work, "It's madness!" Because of the transportation delay, we didn't get to the worksite until around 10:00am, and yet quickly accomplished a lot that morning. I really enjoyed working with Amala and her family all day today. Even though Amala's husband, Ram Babu, wasn't as social as the rest of his family and seemed pretty shy without making much eye contact, that short, petite-built man was an incredible work horse, never tiring, never resting. I don't think he weighed more than 130 pounds soaking wet, and yet I could not believe the amount of shoveling he did, or the weight that he carried on top of his head (I found it very appropriate that his name was Ram). That morning I began to help Amala and her oldest daughter, Anita, mud the bamboo of their house, which was the most enjoyable job I had encountered on the worksite. Ram had dug an 8'x8' hole in the ground, probably 25 yards from their home on the rear of their property. They had already used most of the dirt from that hole to build the foundation for their new home to get it higher than ground level to keep it dry during the rainy season. They had continued to dig down until they reached the level of soil that they were looking for… the dark gray clay that would be mixed and used for mud to cover the inside and outside of the newly built bamboo walls. Even though his body frame was small, Ram had the muscles of a prize fighter, and using a flat head spade he dug up big piles of clay which he had softened with water and then mooshed around with his feet (reminded me of the "I Love Lucy" episode in which Lucy was stomping grapes). He would then dump the dark gray mud off of his spade onto big flat bowls, and when it was your turn in line, he would lift a bowl of mud up and strategically place one on top of your head, perched upon a straw halo for cushion on your skull. While walking up out of the hole and simultaneously balancing the pan on your head to adjust to your body shifting while moving forward, you would follow the worn path along the 25 yards to the rear of their house, where the mooshy clay was dumped off of your head and onto a sheet of plastic (I will always smile when remembering the sound of the clay slapping against the plastic, while jumping back so as not to let it splatter against your shoes and blue jeans). Amala would take handfuls of finely cut straw chaff, add it to the clay/mud mixture and knead it, as if she was making bread, turning it over and over until she had the mud/straw consistency just right. The next step in her process was to section it off and place the clay on big pans, and we would carry it up to the side of the house where it would be applied in a smearing motion across the woven bamboo strips to finish off the walls. Amala and her family were all such amazing

108

people to be around, even though I only understood three words they were saying: pani (PAN-ee) meaning water, muta (MOO-ta), for mud, and dhanyabaad (DHAN-naii-bat) for thank you. They quickly taught me how to spread the mud, and there was a real trick to getting just the right mix of straw, mud and water to make the right concoction. You knew when the mixture was just right because it would actually "splat" when it hit the bamboo after leaving your cupped hand. After you had the mud packed on, then you put water on your hand and smeared it into place. By the time lunch had rolled around, I had gotten pretty skilled at the mudding work as a part of Amala's workforce! Rajesh told me I was lucky, sometimes they used cow dung to do this mudding job, and Larry added if they did that, the Americans would have been puking, to which Rajesh let out one of his Tattoo-da-plane-da-plane belly laughs. Mabel was waiting for us when we got to the lunch area, with her tail wagging as soon as she saw me coming towards her. Today she even allowed me to stroke the top of her head and she took the food right out of my hand (everything in my gut was telling me that she could very easily become an American dog, but how in the heck would I ever get her home (?), and it made me get tears in my eyes just to question that). On our walk back to the worksite after lunch, there was a little boy squatting and pooping right along the side of the road, and he continued to squat like that as we walked by, he wasn't embarrassed or anything (luckily we didn't see any poop drop out the back side or we probably wouldn't have been able to remain serious). Linda and I were then joking that we could have only imagined the things that Bill would have said to him. "Hey kid, are ya lay'n pipe or what?" "How's that work'n out for ya?" "Need a copy of the Times?" The villagers and neighborhood friends of Amala and Bagabati continued to stop by, and Anita (the older sister) began saying their names one by one, as if to introduce me to all of their family friends. I would *try my hardest* to repeat the names exactly as she said them, but inevitably I would somehow screw up the syllables or the

109

pronunciation, which had the whole crowd of onlookers laughing at the red-headed American lady botching up their names. At one point they were all giggling and Amala kept saying, "America, Babita", and Philipe (Jemima's minister-husband who was volunteering with us today) translated for me that Anita jokingly meant that her sister, Babita, would be happy as my daughter in America. At only 13 years of age, and the family's oldest child, Anita was an untiring worker-on-a-mission, just like her parents. I continued to be amazed at how hard she worked, without complaint, and by the end of those days her clothes and skin would be coated with mud and dirt, and yet she was doing this to have a new home (would our teenagers be this willing to work that hard or get that dirty?). Anita cracked me up when at one point, when we were all getting *really* tired and you could tell she had just about had enough mud slinging and mud hauling for one day, she let out an English exasperated, "Oh my God!" I laughed so hard, and then Amala started laughing, then her husband was laughing, then we were ALL laughing. Who would have thought that "Oh my God!" was a universal expression in any language?!? We quit working around 4:30pm, stored our tools away, and all slowly and sorely climbed back on the bus to head back to town (seemed like we continued to do more laborious tasks with each passing day). Our regular route to the village was blocked with a sugar cane wagon loaded about 25 feet into the air, so we backed up and took the bumpier road back into town. Milan wasn't with us today because of the bus strike, so Doc hopped up from his seat, moved into the doorway of the bus and began to hang outside of the bus, banging on the door to scare the animals out of the way of the bus. Dependra jerked his head over to see who was banging on the bus door, and then he got a big chuckle seeing that it was Doc, covering for Milan! Doc did a great job as pseudo door-banger, but we weren't sure he should quit his career as a physician any time soon! It was so funny! As we reached one of the main roads leaving the village, we were met by the police escort for our safe return back into the city since the bus strike was still in full swing. They led us on the highway for about 10 minutes, and then we had to pull over when we came to the end of their jurisdiction to wait for the next set of police to show up and escort us the rest of the way to the hotel (siren on and lights flashing, as if we weren't *already* having enough attention drawn to us). Due to our previous plans to attend a local wedding reception now askew without secure transportation to get there because of the bus strike, we settled for the safety of our dinner routine together at the hotel that evening. We also spent collective time trying to figure out which song we were going to sing on Thursday during the home dedication ceremony. We all unanimously agreed that Phil was going to lead us by singing the Yale University, "Whiffenpoof Song" (we would join him during the Baa! Baa! Baa! chorus), and then we would all sing "Take Me Out to the Ballgame" too. Lots of laughs were had by all during this choir-practice session, and we all turned in early after a very hard day at the worksite, weaving, sand hauling, mud hauling-and-plastering.

Chapter 13

Wednesday, January 26, 2011

Yes, the bus strike was over! Linda and I woke up around 5:30am, before the alarm went off, and we immediately started to hear the bus horns honking on the street in front of the Ratna, so we knew we were back in business! The day was pre-planned for all of us to have breakfast early just in case we had to walk to the police station again like the previous day, so we were ahead of schedule for the morning. In preparation for the ride to the country on these treacherous streets with the strike ending, Doc motioned the sign of the cross on his chest as we pulled away from the hotel. I told him that my friend, Dan Green, had once instructed me that wasn't the sign of the cross, that instead, those were the four things that a man has to check as he's walking into church, "glasses, zipper, watch, wallet". Ha-ha. Several of us noticed this guy who appeared to be carrying a flat bowl full of trash, dodging traffic to run to dump it out on the other side of the street instead of dumping it in front of his own business. That brought on a whole bus discussion about the possibility of whether the trash man only came to one side of the street on certain days?? While typing, I could hear Rajesh sitting in front of me, singing "Majesty" in his native Nepali. He would often sing the same contemporary Christian worship songs that I was familiar with, and it was interesting how I would hear him take off singing a song at the worksite, and even though I couldn't understand the words he was singing, I would know the song that he was singing by recognizing the tune. On our daily bus ride to the countryside, I would sometimes notice poinsettia trees growing along the route, blooming bright red in the dingy environment. They looked just like our Christmas season indoor plants but they had developed and grown into trees, with beautiful blossoms. We stopped at the church and picked up Rajesh's wife and some other volunteers, Kayfur and "Teacher", and since they were taking awhile to walk to the bus, Rajesh quipped, "Show stopper!" That made me smile. Milan (door-banger-extraordinaire) hadn't been with Dependra on the bus for two days now, so Felix jokingly asked Dependra if he had a picture of Milan, so that we could post it on the side of the bus, with a "missing" sign above it. We stopped to buy some tangerines, and across the street from my bus window was a cigarette shop. The sign on the cigarette billboard read, *"Statutory directive: Smoking is injurious to health."* The sky seemed more blue today, everybody was guessing if it was the result of one day without bus pollution in the city! Another very productive day at the worksite became reality, as I spent most of the morning mudding on Amala's house, and then spent time hauling dirt and mud from the deep backyard hole up to the house. At one point, I jumped down into the pit and shoveled like an animal before lunch, and I couldn't remember the last time I had shoveled dirt like that (my back and arm muscles seemed to be wondering the same thing). I continued to be so impressed with how hard these young kids worked. Anita and Babita, and Bagabati's 17-year old daughter, Ranju, worked so hard during the days we were there, they continually carried HUGE loads of dirt or mud on top of their heads and just worked their butts off. The two houses had really taken shape – they wouldn't be totally completed by the final dedication ceremony, but they were now well on their way to being roofed and mudded. I spent the majority of those last two days helping Amala and her family, and it was hard to believe that I would leave there and never see them or their house again. I now understood what these international Habitat for Humanity trips were all about; people brought a part of themselves clear around the world, and then left it behind. I was certain these families would always remember this for the rest of their lives, the winter that "the Americans and Mr. Mexico" came to help them build their homes. We broke for lunch, and walked the jaunt to the lunch area. As usual, there was my Nepal-Mabel, waiting for our arrival. I felt heartsick when I fed her the last bites of my pancakes from my breakfast, carried here in my backpack, for the very last time. After lunch that day, I would never see her again. She took the pancakes, bite by bite, *from my hand,* watching me with those shy brown eyes the whole time, tail wagging. She sat down, and I stroked the top of her precious head. No matter where you go in the world, it's amazing what love can do. Damn, I was such a softie. How did I ever let that bone-thin, stray dog affect my heart that much? Jemima and Nedia made us another great lunch, but when I glanced at Mabel, I didn't have the heart to hardly eat anything. Lunch was soon over, and I somehow made myself walk away while I glanced over my shoulder at Mabel one more time. Wow. That made for a very l-o-n-g walk back to the worksite today. About broke my heart to think that most likely she would show up there tomorrow mid-day at that pavilion with tables and chairs underneath, our lunch spot for the past nine days where a bunch of people had started calling a stray dog "Mabel", and we would be long gone. Back at the worksite, I threw myself into the job at hand and shoveled more than I had in any other day in my 52 years of life, and carried more weight on my head than ever before. I felt there was an unspoken "give it all you've got" mantra, with all of us realizing that these were our last hours to accomplish what we could for these families. I became a mud-hauler, and Bill joined the mudding crew, so I handed him my rubber gloves and he shoved his leather gloves into his back pants pocket, and before I knew it, Bill was inside of Amala's house and had turned into a drip of sweat, laughing and covered with mud. After carrying a few more loads of mud on my head, to dump near the house on the sheet of plastic, Amala pointed that she wanted me back inside of the house to start mudding with Anita, so I went and pulled Bill's leather gloves out of his back pocket, and wore them to mud for the rest of the afternoon (I don't think Bill ever forgave me for ruining his leather gloves, coating them with mud ☺). After our last break of the day (and since this was our last afternoon in the village), Doc spent quite a bit of time "seeing patients" that had lined up for a bit of medical advice. Some of us grabbed our cameras and took off for a walk through the local neighborhood, where I was thrilled to capture some of the best pictures of life in that small village. They were beautiful photographs. I snapped this picture of an elderly woman and her daughter, and it made me wonder what she had seen and been through in her lifetime; her face was weathered with wrinkles, and her skin was like brown leather. She appeared to be blind in one eye or had really bad cataracts, wasn't even sure if she could see the picture of her and her daughter when I showed it to them on my camera screen. We saw a group of men gathered outside of a building, all sitting around in plastic chairs, and we joked, "There is the Elk's Club." The guy that was our HFH construction crew leader for the week (who led us through the village), said that those men were sitting there arranging a marriage. I couldn't imagine my dad choosing my future for me; even if he had chosen my future I guess I hadn't ended up with the man he would have chosen for me anyway, since being divorced 14 years ago. Weird to think about. This was such an enjoyable walk through the rest of the neighborhood. We had worked so hard the past ten days that we had never been out into the village that extended beyond the worksite, and it was meaningful to see these families, up-close and personal. Some of the faces I recognized as those that had been standing and staring at us during the days at the worksite, and they would smile and nod as if to say, "Hello, I remember you and what you did for our community." We circled back to the worksite and cleaned up all of the HFH tools, packing them away in the tool box for the last time. We also threw in there anything that we wanted to donate to HFH and leave behind, work gloves, etc., and headed back to the bus, completing our final day of work (we would be back in the morning, but only for a celebration ceremony with the families to dedicate the houses). I turned around and looked back at the two houses as I neared the bus, and took a final picture for the day, standing in the exact spot where I had snapped the first worksite photo ten days ago. It was amazing to see what our team had accomplished together. What was once a worksite with two bare bamboo pole house frames was now the site of two nearly-completed homes for two very hard-working, well-deserving families. What a difference it makes in the world when people combine their talents and donate time to help others. The ride back to Biratnagar seemed smoggier than ever, good thing we were doing the Himalayan trek in the following days to clear out our lungs. Man, did we all need showers that day when returning to the Ratna! I remember feeling that I had never been dirtier in my entire life!?! We were all either a drip of sweat from hauling dirt or covered with gray clay from slinging mud. Dinner was good as usual, and Rajesh had breaking news and gave a little wrap-up/conclusion speech, thanking us for our time and for everything that we had done in working on the two houses for the past ten days. He added that we hadn't just helped two families gain a better place to live; we had also helped an entire community, by showing them that we were serving with our hearts. We spent the rest of the evening repacking our bags to leave the hotel for the last time the next morning. Our hours in Biratnagar were coming to an end, and that made me very sad ☹.

Chapter 14

Thursday, January 27, 2011

Everybody had breakfast together, our last glorious meal at the Ratna. After discussing our schedule for the day, we all separated. Linda and I headed back upstairs to Room 407 to use the restroom one last time and grab our bags to take them back down to the lobby for our last trip to the worksite and then on to the airport to fly back to Kathmandu. As I lifted my Gander Mountain cargo bag off of the end table where it had been sitting for the past ten days, I about threw up when I discovered a wretched sight. When we had arrived in Biratnagar, Rajesh had adorned us with marigold leis at the airport. When we settled into this room at the Ratna, I had apparently laid our leis (as weird as that sounds) on top of a long glass-covered coffee table. Not even thinking, while unpacking things out of that bag to get it off of the floor for easier use during our stay, I had deposited my bag upon the coffee table, *on top of the leis,* where they unbeknownst to me had remained smooshed underneath that bag for our entire stay. As one might imagine, that had created a GLORIOUS sample of MOLD and FUR on the bottom of my bag and on top of the coffee table both. I about crapped! The site of that Biology 101 mold-fur sample gave Linda and I both a hearty laugh, and Linda proceeded to scrape the rotting marigolds into a trash can, and I quickly washed off the bottom of my bag and the coffee table with a couple of towels which we had deposited onto the slippery bathroom floor for traction after

119

our showers the night before. With that first little adventure of the day behind us, we proceeded downstairs with our luggage, where we found Marilyn and Larry in an accounting-fevered discussion with the hotel manager to settle up our hotel bill for food and lodging for our entire stay. Everyone then proceeded to haul our entire stash of luggage to the curb, and we waited for Dependra and his bus to pick us up at the Ratna for the last time. While standing there waiting in the foggy morning air, clutching Mom's rag rugs for the house dedication ceremony, it was pure enjoyment just watching the city pass by us. Right in the middle of the chaos, I could hardly believe my eyes when coming down the street towards us were two dingy-white burros. It appeared to be a colt with her mother walking behind, slowly passing by (with me, animal-lover extraordinaire, wanting to run out and pet them). We all watched them go by us as we were snapping their picture, with all of us wondering, who do they belong to? Who feeds them? How did they know they were on the correct side of the street to be safe in the flow of traffic? Where were they coming from and where were they headed to? The mother burro kept nudging along the younger colt, and they passed by us and continued right on down the street and disappeared into the morning fog. Our bus arrived, and we slowly loaded our luggage aboard for our departure out of Biratnagar. While traveling through the city and out into the countryside on the way to the worksite for the final time, I struggled to accept the fact that after today, I would realistically never see these two families or any of the friendly villagers again. Little Dashrath was really into the knuckle bump now, *and how could I ever forget Mabel?* It was REALLY foggy during the ride into the countryside, but just about the time we showed up at the worksite, the morning haze evaporated, and it turned out to be a sunny, very warm morning. The dedication ceremony was very nice, and Amala and Bagabati and their families, along with the HFH staff, had decorated their new homes with streamers and balloons, and so many people from the community were there! We had a ribbon-cutting ceremony on each house, and speeches by the JB representative, and Rajesh and Marilyn. We presented each of the families with my mom's gift of a nice thick Amish rag rug, brought here from Indiana, which they gratefully accepted. We closed our stage show in the village with a group song, the Whiffenpoof song. Phil did a grand job of leading the rest of us lost sheep through the "Baa, Baa, Baa" choruses, to the point where watching him stand there and sing the solo parts with his beautiful voice drifting through the air surrounding the two new bamboo houses amidst all of those dark-skinned villagers, brought tears to my eyes. Of course, as far as the village people knew, this just might have been our national anthem or some other religious song. We took lots of photos with both sets of families and our team members, and then tried to separate ourselves with final good-byes. Wow, that was hard, as I had grown attached to the two families, and especially their children. Never, in my wildest imagination, did I ever think I would have traveled to Nepal in my lifetime, yet alone to have been a part of building two bamboo/mud houses in an international Habitat for Humanity global village setting. And now, after spending days there with two Nepalese families (and my new HFH family), building those bonds, I couldn't imagine myself walking away from there either. It was the strangest feeling, and I had a hard time looking at any of them, or telling them good-bye, without my lip trembling and tears rolling. Bottom line, I would never be able to forget their faces, and that was a sad yet warm feeling in my heart. After Doc played community physician again and had a few more almost-patients line up to ask him medical advice, we all loaded back onto Dependra's bus and drove away from the village for the very last time. As I glanced back from my bus window, there was my little buddy Dashrath, running around outside of his new home with his neighborhood buddies. He was chasing them with a long rod of sugar cane, back to life-as-he-knew-it, wearing the same yellow shirt and red sweatpants with a hole in them, that he had on when I saw him for the first time. Had to laugh at him running around like that, and then I wiped back the tears and started typing. We stopped in Biratnagar for a quick visit at the JB office, and we left there after a question that wasn't answered by a yes or no and took what seemed like forever to be answered (which was an inside joke for all of our team members). We then headed to Rajesh's church where Jemima and others had prepared a final going away lunch for us while Doc played doc again (I think if he could have stayed all day, Rajesh would have lined up people to come, as the chance for his church members to receive medical advice was extremely valued). Even though Dependra got us to the airport in plenty of time, the trip to the airport felt like I was in some kind of time tunnel. We had only been there for 11 days, but it felt like months. Working on those homes, getting to spend time with those families, and soaking in all of the laughter and memories that I had experienced with my HFH buds had somehow replaced my regular-life routine, and yet it was like this whole experience was just a long night's dream. We unloaded all of our bags from Dependra's bus, and said good-bye to Rajesh and Dependra one last time. We checked our bags, and then had to spend way too much time, prior to departure, in a waiting room that smelled horribly rank of human urine (i.e. we couldn't get on the plane fast enough). We finally loaded the plane, and took the very scenic flight over the stunning Himalayan mountain range from Biratnagar back to Kathmandu. Puskal, with his familiar friendly face, met us at the airport in a nice shiny van, to which Larry asked of the van itself, "Where have you been for the last week?" Compared to Dependra's bus, that van was a **Cadillac**, and we all laughed in agreement. We wove our way through Kathmandu back to the Hotel Norbu Linka, which was the same Kathmandu hotel that we had stayed in prior to the HFH adventure. We threw our bags in our rooms, and followed our guide to the Fire & Ice Pizzeria, where we had *wonderful* pizza/soup/salads and everybody was very happy to have American food again, accompanied by beer,

122

soda, etc. YUM. OK, maybe double yum. YUM-YUM. Upon returning to the hotel, everybody sat in the lobby and settled up to prepay the cost of the five-day Himalayan trek that we were about to embark on the next morning. Pascul took our cash or our credit cards, and gave us all receipts and got everybody lined up for the trek pick-up the following day. Raya Tours provided us with red canvas duffle bags to pack our trek belongings into, so the porters would have all-the-same-size-of-bags to carry on their backs. There would only be nine of our HFH team crazy enough to attempt the trek adventure, as Larry and Cheryl had already previously planned to head back to the States after the HFH build was completed, as they had a new grandbaby to go see! Everybody was frustrated because we couldn't get the internet connection to work prior to going to bed, so we all gave up, thinking maybe in the morning?? We took a quick shower; MAN, the water was SCALDING hot. Unlike Biratnagar, where the hot was on the right, the knobs here would lead you to believe that the hot is on the right, but the hot is on the left. How is a person supposed to know these things? Ha-ha. I sat up and read for a while, and finished the book that I brought with me to read on this trip, "Barefoot" by Elin Hilderbrand. What a cute story, and I threw it across the room to Linda so she could read it on her flight home. I then began to work on taking everything out of my Gander Mountain bag to prepare for the Himalayan trek, putting only the trek items needed for the next five days into my Raya Tours duffel bag (and storing everything else back in the cargo bag). The Norbu Linka management was gracious enough to let us store our non-needed-pre-trek suitcases there in a storage room while we were away trekking, so after setting aside everything I thought I wouldn't need to haul along on the trek, I TRIED to get some sleep. It was freezing cold in that room, but the bed there was certainly softer than the one in Biratnagar (and there was no mouse sighting – BONUS!).

Chapter 15

Friday, January 28, 2011

Our whole team met downstairs for breakfast in the hotel's small café, and we all said our final farewells to Larry and Cheryl, as they were flying out the next day and would not be heading to Pokhara to start the trek with us that morning (the eleven would become nine). After some hugs and tearful good-byes with Larry and Cheryl (and boy, could that warm-hearted-farmer-guy Larry give a big hug), the Raya Tour guides picked up the remaining soon-to-be trekkers in our group and took us in their big van to the Kathmandu airport to catch the Yeti Airlines 25-minute flight to Pokhara, where we would officially start the trek on Saturday morning. That seemed like a very short flight, but it would have taken HOURS to drive that route through the mountain range. After landing in Pokhara, we were met at the airport by our trek guides for the next several days, Krishna Chhetri and his faithful sidekick, Mint. We spent most of that day sightseeing around Pokhara, which seemed like a much cleaner, less polluted city than Biratnagar. I remember thinking to myself that if I ever came back to Nepal this is where I would want to visit again (besides a quick trip to see our adopted Biratnagar families, of course). We stopped at Devi's Falls, which would have been a lot prettier during the monsoon season (the river was pretty dry and held back by a dam on the lake). The trash around this tourist area was so hard for all of us to get accustomed to (and those that lived around Pokhara would have been blown away if ever given the chance to witness the enormity of the Niagara Falls). Our next stop was cave exploring at the Gupteshwor Cave, which was really pretty cool. It was like the Ohio Caverns, less the stalactites and stalagmites ☺. I kept thinking while we were climbing down the flights of dark, damp stairs heading into the cave that this was just a pre-cursor to what might lie ahead of us in the coming days, and they were just using this as a practice run to see if we could all pass this physical test. The lights went out when we were in the cave, so everyone was ordered to stand very still (which left us slightly panicked) as it was BLACK with no lighting. The lights soon came back on and we eventually reached the waterfall where we attempted to take pictures of the falls in an area darker than Batman's cave. We climbed back to the top of the cave and out into the warm sunshine, and sat for a rest. We walked to meet the bus and continued on to a Tibetan Refugee Camp and monk area, where we did a little shopping, and then proceeded to the Hotel Panorama, where we would stay prior to the trek departure the following morning. The sides of the steps leading up to the hotel lobby were adorned with countless flower pots filled with blooming red and pink geraniums and Gerbera daisies… we hadn't seen blooming flowers for months back in Indiana! It was delightful! The hotel had a beautiful, marble-lined staircase but freezing cold rooms, and it didn't help that without noticing, my roomie Linda and I had slept with a window open all night and were awakened by a crowing rooster in the morning around 5:00am. Ha-ha.

Chapter 16

Saturday, January 29, 2011

We were up bright and early, our first official trekking day! After breakfast I quickly brought my duffel bag downstairs, and sat outside in the sun on the steps, and enjoyed the scent of the geraniums all around me. Since I lived in Indiana in the midst of a snowy winter, it would be another four or five months before I would get to smell growing flowers again! Krishna, Mint and our four porters for the trek arrived to pick us up, and soon we were on our way to Kasyari with all of our Raya Tours red duffel bags secured with ropes on the top of the van. We were driven outside of Pokhara, along a winding road which ran out into some dry rice paddies, and we all piled out of the van and began to help unload all of our bags. The morning haze was burning off and the temperature was moving up the thermometer, so some of us peeled a layer of hiking clothes and quickly tucked them into our bags before Krishna, Mint, and the four young porters separated the bags and figured out amongst them who was going to carry what to keep the loads equal. With our weighed-down porters leading the way with our bags attached to their backs, we started the trek by crossing over a small creek, and began the ascent into the lower mountain foothills. It was amazing to see those four young men, carting all of the weight of our bags (Krishna and Mint were guides and not porters). They had magically laced the bags together with rope, and then tied a band to the bags, which they would support using their forehead and neck muscles with the band (which looked like it should have been padded with sheepskin or cotton padding, but it wasn't). I couldn't believe the beginning uphill ascent, it had my heart beating very rapidly; so much for thinking that getting up and riding my spinner bike every morning at 5:30am for weeks in advance had physically prepared me for this trek! Maybe it was just the altitude that I wasn't accustomed to, or the fact that it had been almost ten years since I had hiked the Grand Canyon with Young Dendinger and Mike, all of which ran through my mind while listening to my heartbeat! I had started the trek with long underwear under my hiking pants to help with the chill in the morning air, but by the first morning break, I had already warmed up enough to remove the long underwear, standing behind a rock wall separating two fields, out of the view of my fellow trekkers. I spent the rest of the day in a long-sleeve shirt and my hiking capris, my hiking boots and a pair of both cotton and wool hiking socks, and was plenty warm. We climbed upward, along rock-covered pathways, every once in a while climbing over wooden fences and stopping along the way to snap shots of beautiful terraced views of the flat lands that we were quickly leaving behind. It was funny… Doc, Deb and I (and their friend, Kevin Miller), had made a trip to the huge Cabela's store in Dundee, Michigan, prior to this Nepal adventure to buy wind-sheer coats for this trek, and now it appeared the temperatures were going to be in the upper 60's or lower 70's by mid-afternoon on every day of the trek. For the duration of this trip, I continued to be sooooo thankful to have that coat along though, because even though I didn't wear it during the day, it was *extremely valuable* to help keep my body from freezing once the sun went down each night. We stopped several times for breaks along the way that morning, hiking through beautiful small Nepali villages; all of the people were so friendly and would share their welcoming "Namaste" with accompanying smiles and folded hands. We passed through a village where a group of men were playing cards, and Phil got a charge out of me quipping, "Got any 2s?

Go fish!" I always enjoyed seeing the different dogs in the villages, and when I stopped to pet one of them sporting a wagging tail, Mint said to me, "He's an honest dog" (the translation of their language to ours often brought a smile to my face). We continued our climb towards Kalikasthan, and most of us were exhausted by mid-afternoon when we reached the destination of Day #1 of the trek. We would be housed that evening in our first family home on a "hilltop" (what a heck of a hill!) with the nicest Nepali family. It was funny seeing everyone gradually one by one reach the vista which overlooked a huge valley below, collapsing onto the ground, lying on straw mats or sitting up at a picnic table. After an hour or so of resting, the family, along with guidance from Krishna and Mint, prepared a nice lunch, along with beers, colas, or whatever we needed. Their children were adorable, and the little girl of the family, who appeared to be about four-years old, was very bright, and I shared my chocolate bar with her which she LOVED. She knew the English alphabet, and later in the evening would chime in with letter-knowledge when our team and the porters were all engrossed in the nightly Bananagrams game (we might have left a hundred things back in our bags at the hotel in Kathmandu, but heaven help us if we didn't have Steve's Bananagrams game along!! – we were officially addicted!). I was shocked to see cell towers and power lines at this altitude; in fact we were all able to take turns charging our cameras from an electric plug which was strung along a wood beam in the room that the Egli's bunked in, hung from above their beds. After lunch we all had a chance to stretch out in the sun on the straw mats, and it was hilarious to see everybody soaking in the sun. At one point I looked around and thought we looked like a bunch of cats stretching and purring, everybody rubbing their feet and sore leg muscles. It was amazing how quickly it cooled down once the sun set, we were all running for more layers of clothes. Everyone got settled into their assigned rooms, and for this first night's stay on the trek, Linda, Marilyn and I all bunked in one room. The room was barely big enough for three tiny, thin, less-than-twin-size mattresses setting atop wooden slats, and we rolled out our trekking-company-supplied nylon sleeping bags for the first time. Prior to dinner, in what I believe was a self-inflicted effort to stay warm, all nine of us squeezed into the "guys" room, which was made up of three twin beds and housed Bill, Phil and Steve (the Egli's were in another room). All nine of us were sitting on three twin beds, telling adventures from our lives. I shared with everybody my friend Judi's battle with cancer, and what an inspiration she was to me on this climb. I was so thankful to physically attempt this trek, and I was doing it for **both** Judi and myself - no matter how fast my heart beat and how sore my muscles were, I would not give up! It was really cold (kept thinking to myself THIS was what we bought those Cabela's coats for!), and even with nine of us shivering together for warmth in this room, and me wearing as many layers as I could get on, with gloves, etc., I don't think I ever did warm up that night. It was dark by the time we had dinner (tomato soup, fried rice, potatoes and vegetables), but it was amazing to see them cook our dinner over a fire in a one-room kitchen that was so smoke-filled that I couldn't breathe when taking a picture. I'm sure it also had a lot to do with the cow dung or wood they were using for fire fuel in an unventilated internal kitchen. It quickly dawned on me that there was no way of getting around having to poop over a squat pot for the next four days and three nights, so I eventually succumbed to natural bodily functions and grinned and bared it (literally), giggling the whole time. I continued to be amazed, at how on this trip, the once-strange, quickly became the-norm. I got pretty efficient at balancing myself, tearing off toilet paper, keeping my pants or pajama bottoms or boots from getting splashed with anything and getting the job done, all while holding my flashlight with my teeth. Yeah Kaysie! That night was interesting, sleeping on that flat bed, zipped in a V-shaped nylon sleeping bag, tossing and turning like a lobster in a pot of hot water. During the middle of the night I swore I was dreaming about neon nights, and then realized it was the reflection of Marilyn's flashlight on the ceiling of the room. I helped her locate my flashlight since the beam on mine was bigger, and she was off to the squat pot. Later on during the night while flipping over, my "pillow" which felt like a piece of thick cardboard covered with a bath towel, slid off of the slippery sleeping bag, hit the floor, and I let out an out loud "holy crap". There was no way I was falling back to sleep after that, and my mind started to roll. I flashback'd to earlier that evening when the nine of us one-day-under-our-belts trekkers, were all sitting together in the guys bunk room, and how I had told them about my friend, Judi. And then, in the wee morning hours, it felt like I replayed my friendship with Judi year by year, memory by memory, flying through my head. "Jude", her shortened nickname, and I had met when we were working in the automotive world in 1995, she in the Sales Department and me in the Inquiry Department at Cooper in Auburn. During that time I had hit a plateau in my life where I wasn't really sure who I was any more. I had been married for 17 years, with a nice husband and two unbelievably great kids, and we lived the all-American dream in an all-American house in an all-American city, but as weird as it might sound, I felt like my life wasn't mine, as if I was living in someone else's dream world. I had a close knit circle of married friends whose ages stretched across almost every decade of working-life in that office, some older than me, some younger than me, and there wasn't anything that I was facing in life that one of those women hadn't already been through and survived in their past. Judi, though divorced twice previously, was head-over-heels-crazy-in-love with a new man in her life, Howie, who was ten years her junior. They eventually were married at his 40th birthday party, to which, *unbeknownst to Howie,* Judi had already invited close friends and family, AND a justice of the peace to perform their marriage ceremony. The JP had previously agreed to take the job with three stipulations: Jude required that the justice... 1) had to be able to legally marry them, 2) he had to feel free to drink with everybody at the party, *and* 3) he had to be able to sing karaoke. Right then and there, in their back yard under a tall pine tree, she asked him to marry her and they tied the knot that had survived the test of time. Fast forward in our friendship to the fall of 2009, when Judi began to have what she thought were back spasms, which were eventually diagnosed as seizures. This led to 18 months of an unbelievable nightmare and one of the biggest challenges of Judi's entire life. In November, at Bruce Buttermore's 40th birthday party, in the lobby of a local eatery, I saw Jude seize for the very first time. During the party, she and Howie had left the room when she felt the seizure coming on, and I caught up with them out in a hallway. I sat beside Jude while she talked to me throughout the entire maybe three-minute seizure that seemed like a 30-minute, unbelievable bad dream to me. Her entire body violently bounced off of a wooden chair, with her right leg extended straight out, and she continually denied my pleas to call for some assistance. She kept saying it was just a back spasm like others that she had previously experienced, but admitted to me afterwards that the "spasms" were happening more frequently. The final straw and the turning point to begin the search for more answers to her growing list of odd physical maladies came when Judi had a seizure during a class she was taking at a Fort Wayne college campus to complete her bachelor's degree. The seizure was bad enough that they had to call her daughter Dawn, to come pick up Judi and drive her home. A visit to the family doctor ensued the next day, which was followed by ordered visits to an imaging center. A pain management specialist ran tests with electrodes on her right leg (as she silently knew she didn't have a lot of feeling remaining in her right leg at that point anyway). After another huge seizure in the parking lot of her son's automotive body shop in Angola, she regained consciousness with all three of her adult children (Perry, Chad and Dawn) and Howie staring at her, which left her feeling like a circus show. They drove her to the doctor's office, which was followed by visits to a neurologist, and then an oncologist. By the time

132

Thanksgiving rolled around, Judi thought she remembered knowing she had cancer, but it was all just a blur. The Wednesday after Thanksgiving, at a doctor's appointment in Auburn, she remembers being told to go home, get ready, and immediately go to Lutheran Hospital in Fort Wayne. She and Howie went home, fed "the girls" (two Shih Tzu puppies, Mokie and Maggie) and then went straight to Lutheran, where she was scheduled to have surgery the next morning to remove a tumor located in the left frontal lobe portion of her brain. Judi described it as being such an unbelievable, deniable experience, as if it just couldn't have been reality. Once situated in her room at the hospital, they started bringing her release papers that she had to sign prior to the surgery, she called them "release if you think you're gonna die papers" (i.e. living will paperwork). She remembers telling Howie and Dawn to fill out the papers however it suited them, that she didn't care. If they thought she was gonna live, then she wanted them to resuscitate her. But if they thought she wasn't going to live, then she didn't want them to bother because she didn't want her chest beat on. The brain surgery was on a Thursday, but she never came back to reality until Sunday, and when she did, she had debilitating muscular damage to the right side of her body (with limited use of her arm and hardly any use of her right leg). Even though she had gone through the brain surgery, she had yet to understand the reality of her situation – the tumor in her brain had metastasized from a tumor in her lungs. The lung tumor was possibly a result from the years when Judi herself would say she was a smoking fool (even though she had quit smoking years before the cancer was diagnosed). The following Wednesday after her surgery, Judi remembers someone coming into her room with information on the Cancer Society, and they proceeded to explain to her what was happening to her body. She had no clue what she was facing, and at that point she didn't even realize that because of the limited use of her right leg, she would be wheelchair-bound until further therapy. And when the therapy people did come to visit her, Judi remembers being really pissed off at that point, because how dare some therapy person come into her room and tell her that she was going to be in a wheelchair, and that she wasn't going to be able to walk. She had been using an adult potty chair beside her hospital bed which they had assisted her during the use of, so it never occurred to her that she wouldn't have mobility at home, and would need to be in a wheelchair?? She remembered they had gotten her up and had assisted her in learning to use a walker with a band strapped around her waist, but she wasn't mentally clear enough at that point to understand that her leg wasn't functioning because the tumor and subsequent surgery had affected the right side of her body. She never put it together that she wasn't going to walk. The day she was released from the hospital in a wheelchair, she had an appointment at an imaging center where a whole-body PET scan was done to check her body for cancer cells. She went home, and in the days ahead, she had a follow-up appointment with her neurologist. He told her that she had already beaten the odds, as 90% of the patients that had a tumor like hers, as big as hers was and in the spot hers was located, did not survive to make it back to their first follow-up appointment. A few days later, she received a letter in the mail from her oncologist's office, outlining all of the appointments that she would need prior to starting the first of 14 radiation treatments on her brain. She shared that the first initial visit to the oncologist's office was so surreal, she wondered, how could *she* have cancer? She was wild, free-spirited Judi, and suddenly she was left with a body that was wheelchair-bound, unable to use her right side as she once did, with a scar across the top of her head. How could this have happened to her? A nurse came into her examination room and compassionately explained a lot of stuff, but Judi just remembers falling apart, and crying non-stop. Judi said they tried to convince her to be a part of a good cancer support group, but Judi explained to me that when your life was turned upside down like that, you hated feeling like you were dependent upon your family and friends to take you to these group meetings as everybody was busy and you didn't want to intrude on their lives. And then, as Judi so lovingly tells people, she got to the place where she was a being a pain-in-the-ass to everyone. She was so angry and bitter with the hand that she had been dealt, that her family couldn't put up with her anymore, which led to Howie and Dawn putting her in the car one day and driving her to the doctor. Judi said by the time they were called back to the examination room, they were all in tears because they just didn't know how to handle the whole cancer nightmare that had taken over their lives. She said the doctor came in, took one look at the three of them, and with his precedent knowledge of their current situation, he sat down on the examination stool and rolled right up to Judi. Right at her level, looking at her eye-to-eye with his hand upon her knee, he asked her what was wrong. Judi said she remembers smiling through her tears and answering back, "I'm not sure, but I think *they* all have issues." Through the laughter, the doctor then said to Judi, "So I should be treating *them*?" And Judi said, "Yes." They all chuckled and talked through all of their "issues", and he reassured them that he could help by prescribing some drugs for Judi to emotionally help her with everything happening to her (and her family) on this journey. Jude will be open to tell you that when you or someone you love gets a cancer diagnosis, it takes a long time to figure it all out for yourself. She said that once she accepted the fact that she had stage-4 brain cancer, she could then face that diagnosis and have the attitude with the doctor and Howie, as if to say, it is what it is, and whatever I have to do to keep living is fine with me. She said that didn't mean that those brave thoughts were coming from her heart, because inside she was so damned scared. More scared than anything in her lifetime, she said it was like the kiss of death. And so the radiation therapy began on her brain. Judi's mom would drive from Fort Wayne to Auburn and pick her up on the mornings that she had radiation (because without the use of her right leg, Judi couldn't drive nor maneuver the wheelchair for long distances).

Her mom would drive Judi back into Fort Wayne for her treatments, which was sometimes days in a row. Judi's mom, who at age 78, and as Judi so eloquently puts it, "drives like her ass is on fire", would most days have Judi worried that she *wasn't going to live as a result of her mother's driving until she reached the doctor's office.* Judi said the radiation therapy began each session by her putting on a mask that had been previously fitted and created for her own head to block out the radiation rays to certain areas, and then she would be laid down on a table, where that mask would be fastened to the table to prevent her head from moving during the treatment. A big machine similar to a CT scan would be lowered from the ceiling, with red painless radiation beams criss-crossing in all directions in 5–10 minute sessions, pinpointed to the cancerous area in her brain, leaving her flush and red in the face from the radiation being shot into her body. During this time and for the coming months, like a lot of cancer patients, she closed down the world-of-Judi... she avoided all phone calls and all email, she didn't want to deal with the questions that would come from talking to anybody. After radiation came the process of trying to combat the cancerous tumor in her lung, for which her oncologist pushed the insurance company to move forward with the Cyberknife surgery at Parkview, that he wasn't waiting on the insurance approval for that procedure and that he was going ahead with it anyway (her oncologist will forever be her hero). The oncologist told her he was lining her up with the best fiducial placement points person they had at Parkview, and soon she had points inserted into her chest cavity to mark her lung tumor. The compassionate care that she received from a Parkview radiology nurse (who said if the weather would have been nicer, she would have taken Judi to the ice cream shop down the street) will never be forgotten. She had the three Cyberknife treatments in February (four days apart), which took several hours each time (she said she felt her entire body was radiated, even though she knows it was pinpointed to a certain area), and then she was granted a break from any treatments during the month of March because her thin body just couldn't take any more. And just like we all knew she would, with her kick-ass-attitude, Jude kept going. The sessions of chemotherapy to battle her lung cancer then began in April and ran all the way through the end of June. By that time she would say that she was nothing but a rack of bones, with all of her hair and every extra ounce of weight falling off of her body in rapid succession. From the minute her eyes opened every morning, she would already be dry-heaving from the chemo long before she hung her head over the toilet and she would just continually cry because she was so non-stop sick. She took Zophran to help battle the nausea, but any scent in the house would have her throwing up again (Howie got to the point where he ate every one of his meals away from home, because Judi would get nauseous whenever he cooked). Her sense of smell kicked into high gear and practically took over her life, eliminating every free minute of normal existence and leaving her weak and continually sick to her stomach. I remember stopping at Judi and Howie's country ranch-style house early one Sunday morning while circling back towards Auburn on a 25-mile bike ride to get ready for the September Huntington Bicycle Challenge. I walked down the hallway of their home towards their bedroom and Howie got me a chair so I could sit beside the bed and talk. Judi was propped up in their bed, so weak and thin, with only a few wisps of her beautiful blonde hair remaining on her nearly bald head. As was the norm between Jude and me, she had me laughing in no time, and I countered her laughter by cracking her up with me telling her that my bike-sweaty-butt was going to leave a mark on her wooden chair. I glanced at the scar that went from side to side on the top of her head, and knew that her determination made her stronger than I could ever hope to be. Even though her body was weak and she was waging an all-out-war both mentally and physically with the cancer in her body, in her at-times-tearing eyes I still saw that Judi-I-can-kick-your-butt spirit that reassured me that she had accepted it, BUT *she was never giving up.* That day we talked about how we ALL live on borrowed time. From the minute we're born until the day that our souls leave this beloved earth, we are ALL living on borrowed time. Our lives are a gift from God, that we in a sense are borrowing, and would one day give back to Him, laid at his feet. Within that Sunday morning hour of talking with Judi, she healed my heart that had been scarred with an unhealed wound, the result of a misunderstanding with a friend who years earlier had lost his battle with cancer. That friend had closed down parts of his life, and he died without ever talking to me again. I had carried that sadness for years, and yet in that hour of seeing cancer thru Judi's eyes, her understanding and translation of how he must have felt, patched that hurt in my heart. I left her house that morning with a new understanding of how a cancer patient sees life and reacts to things that happen differently than do those who tend to take their life for granted. Judi had found a new way of accepting her altered life, and she now saw every day with unbridled clarity and a new-found gift for living in the moment. She was the strong one, and I was inspired just to be around her. With each month her spirit and body grew stronger, and she learned to maneuver around via a wheelchair, until with therapy and a constant leg brace, she eventually regained the use of her right leg to be mobile with only a cane. Jude was never giving up on life, and I was never giving up on her. And there I was, on a Himalayan trek, trying to sleep on a rock hard bed in a house on the side of a mountain in Nepal, clear on the other side of the world, thinking about Jude. She was still battling her cancer, but I laughed at that hideous cancer for *even thinking* about taking on that woman! Our lives only last for such a short time on this earth, how dare we ever take one minute for granted? Borrowed time. Judi always says that you had better be thankful for everything you've got, and that even with everything she had been through, she was never giving up on her faith. What a great gift God had given me in the blessings of my friends. I was so thankful that the journey of my life and this trip to Nepal had led me to that very moment. I finally drifted off to sleep, trying to imagine what tomorrow would bring.

Chapter 17

Sunday, January 30, 2011

We all had early wake up calls (i.e. the trek guides pounding on the little wooden doors of our rooms), in order to get up early enough to see the sun rise on to the mountains. It was absolutely stunning! We took lots of pictures and I was in awe of the sun hitting the snow-covered peaks of the Annapurna mountain range and turning everything a beautiful pink. Everybody was slightly stiff and sore from Day #1, which was quite a work-out, and climbing that steeply right out of the gate was an adjustment to the altitude change too. Nothing like a morning trip to the squat toilet, using a wet-wipe for a whore's bath on your girly parts when it's about 45 degrees out, brushing your teeth outside while rinsing your teeth and toothbrush with bottled water and spitting onto the ground, combing your hair and throwing it back in a headband, putting on deodorant, a new T-shirt and new underwear, and feeling like a new girl! We rolled up our sleeping bags, repacked our duffel bags and day packs, which included dumping more bottled water into the camel reservoir in my backpack to get ready for the day's hike. After a breakfast of warm porridge with fruit, eggs, and flat bread covered with peanut butter, we said good-bye to our host family and took off. We walked along the ridge of the mountain and then the trek trail descended down through a beautiful terraced valley, and wound through old settled villages with quaint thatched-roofed homes and gardens. Marilyn had on a long-sleeved T-shirt during the morning trek, and she soon warmed up during the morning hike. At her request, Doc got out a scalpel blade and gave it to Linda so she could cut off Marilyn's shirt sleeves for her. Shirt surgery at its finest! We always had snacks at the morning break stops, usually fruit (bananas, apples, tangerines), plus chocolates or other trail mix snacks that we had purchased in Pokhara and packed for the trek. Phil's 72-year old knee was beginning to bother him, so Doc got into his magic bag of tricks and handed him an ace bandage to wrap his knee with. While Bill was standing in front of Phil, so Phil could take down his pants and wrap his knee in a little privacy, Bill quipped in, "Phil hurry up and pull up your pants, you're scaring the horses." There was certainly never a dull moment with those guys around; they were hilarious the entire trip. I got so hot at one point during the hike that I felt sick to my stomach and had to go behind some bushes and trees out of sight and take a quick pit stop. That was a new experience for me, pooping out in the middle of freakin' nowhere. Luckily I never went anywhere without a roll of toilet paper in my backpack (trekkers rule #1), so afterwards, I put a big rock on top of the toilet paper, and then laughed out loud at myself for doing that (I'm really not sure why I did that, but it seemed an eco-friendly-efficient-thing to do at that moment). We were originally scheduled to spend the night in Syaklung, but when Krishna did the pre-trek work of arranging for homes for us to stay in, he couldn't find sufficient housing there, so instead we ended up spending the evening in the village of Lipeyani, where the inn won the "cleanest squat toilet" award of the trek in our book (as if that was saying a lot). After our second day of completed trekking, the beers and Cokes never tasted so good, and I ate more at this late afternoon lunch than any other meal on the trek. Krishna and Mint were not only good guides, but they were cooking gurus too, and helped prepare every meal that we had along the way. For lunch they fixed rice (now there's a shocker), potatoes and cauliflower, and bread that was fried flat, like a spicy white crunchy tortilla shell with some after-heat spice. I could tell that I had lost weight on this trip already because my jeans seemed to get looser every day when I put them on at night for warmth. My guess is that had a lot to do with the workout and the amount of sweating we did each day, and also because I just hadn't been eating as much during the home build as I did back in the States. While tucking away our bags and sleeping bags into our second floor assigned room for Trek-Night-#2, Linda and I both **whacked** our heads on our room's low doorway header *countless* times when going in or out of our tiny sleeps-two-in-twin-beds room (I recall hearing **"Oh cuss!"** said a few times), and then Linda even whacked hers again on the bamboo rod that was running across our room ceiling (I can close my eyes and giggle at the memory of the sound of my head smashing into that door-header). With the sun still high in the sky after our late lunch, the majority of us grabbed straw mats and headed up to the terrace behind the inn and took wonderful cat naps in the sun. Bill wasn't feeling so well, and ended up being very sick with signs of a fever, etc., and he went into his bed-for-the-night and got into his coat and sleeping bag to sweat it off (Doc gave him some good drugs and he slept for several hours). The evening meal was also good – chicken soup and chicken fried rice, and we sat around a campfire and the porters sang songs for us and did local Nepali dances. Bill woke up around 9:00pm and came out to the campfire feeling so much better, which was a huge relief to all of us because we had all been concerned and wondered how we would get him back to Pokhara if he was still sick the next morning. I felt myself falling asleep while watching the campfire, so I told everyone good-night and headed to our room. When I got back to the room, I found my flashlight and returned outdoors to brush my teeth and visit the squat pot one more time. When I went back to our room and closed the door behind me, I turned to see this HUGE dead spider body hanging from a web on the back of the door, which scared the behjeeesus out of me and I screamed. Sooooo, when Linda came back to the room a short while later, we did a high-tech flashlight scan of the entire room, found more dead spider bodies, and then Linda proceeded to squash a lovely spider that was *still alive* (AAGGHH!), terminating its life with her shoe (it was reddish-brown and gross!). I ended the day by climbing WAY DOWN into my sleeping bag with the hood of my Parkview Don't Text and Drive sweatshirt tied *tightly around my chin,* fearing revenge-of-the-huge-spiders all night long. It seemed like I tossed and turned a lot, the wooden bed frame was concrete-hard and seemed to moan and groan every time I rolled over (the bed, not me, even though my muscles were getting a darn good workout on this trek!). I got up in the middle of the night and made a squat pot trip, and when I was done, I left the outhouse and stood on the terrace where we had sunned ourselves earlier in the day. Couldn't believe what I was seeing, as I was in awe of the world's canopy above me. The entire sky of the planet <u>for as far as I could see</u> was blanketed in solid stars. I had never experienced a night sky so star-filled, *from on top of the world* like that. What an awesome God we serve. I will never forget turning off the flashlight to soak in the entire sky, just in awe of where I was at, and thinking about my family on the other side of the world, with not a sound to be heard. Total silence. And there I was, in the middle of the Himalayan Mountains without a clue as to what time it was, no idea where I was on the map, on a hillside in the dead of night, under a canopy of stars, not a soul around, except me and God, just hanging out. The lyrics of a Chris Tomlin song, "Indescribable", seemed to play in my head... "From the highest of heights to the depths of the sea, creation's revealing Your majesty, from the colors of fall to the fragrance of spring, every creature unique in the song that it sings. All exclaiming, indescribable, uncontainable, *You placed the stars in the sky and You know them by name,* You are amazing, God." I had never been that humbled in His greatness in my entire lifetime, and at that moment, there was not a lot of earth in between us. He was everywhere and everything, as if time did not exist, and I was thankful to just be standing there by myself in silence. I'm not really sure how long I stood there, gazing at the stars, but I eventually made myself walk down the stairs from the terrace and sneak back into our room. I quietly climbed back into Spiderville, and finally fell asleep.

Chapter 18

Monday, January 31, 2011

Woke up only-God-knows-when to the sounds of roosters while it was still dark as the ace of spades. Didn't roosters know how to tell time over there? You had to be kidding me! I tried to fall back asleep, but soon heard Doc pounding on our door for a wake up call to get up and see the sunrise. I threw on my coat and several warmer layers of clothes and sprinted up the mountain behind the terrace to take pictures of the sunrise hitting the Annapurna mountain range that stretched out in front of us. It was absolutely stunning, and we were so thrilled that we were able to capture this view so early in the morning without fog. While we were waiting for breakfast to be prepared in the kitchen of the inn, it was nice to take in the surrounding village morning bustle. There were children walking to school, and then we had to listen to the sounds of what-we-were-pretty-sure were two small goats being castrated in the shop right across the street from our breakfast table (as Tina would say, "O.M.G."). Bill was back to his ornery self, bright-eyed and bushy-tailed at the breakfast table, which was so good to see. After we finished with breakfast and we were in the process of loading up all of our gear to proceed on the trek for the day, the owner of the inn anointed our foreheads with what appeared to be oatmeal-birdshit as a blessing (the concoction was actually rice and yogurt, and then he also put a scarf around our neck to bless the rest of our journey). It was a weird feeling to have that cold wet stuff dripping off of your forehead and onto your nose and running down your cheek, and stand there while people were talking to you. We were passed this morning on the path by some school children, and Krishna told us that some of these kids walked two hours one way to school each day (talk about a desire to attend school?!?). Mint and Krishna had warned us ahead of time that today would be the most difficult day on the five-day trek, and I had to agree with their perception. There were points I would pause to let my heart take a break and catch my breath, and when I stopped I would always grab my camera from where I had handily tied it to my backpack, and bring it up to eye-level because I just had to record the scenery that we were hiking through. Beautiful stone-paved ascents, overlooking the mountains and valleys surrounding us. During the mid-morning break, I asked Krishna if I could attempt to pick up and carry (on my own back) one of the loads that the porters were carrying. The porters began to shake their heads no, as if they were saying that the loads were too heavy for me to try that. Finally I acted out the Popeye-strong-muscles-curl, so they helped me load one of their strapped packs onto my back and fit the brace strap across my forehead to help bear the weight of the load. They stood back but remained very close in case my body buckled under the weight, and I will NEVER forget how heavy that load was. That experiment gave me a whole new *unbelievable appreciation* for those four young men, hauling those packs up and down those mountains, especially on the wet steps and slippery terrain that we sometimes navigated. The weight was almost unbearable, and to know they could also balance that and not tip forward, backwards or sideways was unimaginable. Seemed like I was able to handle that load for a whole whopping 20 seconds, and then I began to grimace so they quickly unloaded it from my back, and helped Marilyn try it on so she could experience that also. Wow. After that morning break, we proceeded up the mountainside on what I felt was the steepest ascent of the entire trek. I guessed it to be about

148

600m straight up, scaling back and forth in sharp switchbacks, right up the side of the mountain. My heart was beating so hard, and by the time we crested to a plateau, I was really out of breath. Phil and Bill were the last to arrive to the top, so the team made an "Amazing Race" body tunnel, and everybody congratulated them when they walked through, which was very cool. I continued to be so impressed with Bill, Phil and Steve, throughout the entire trek. Those guys were older than me by 20 years, and yet they kept right up, moved forward, sometimes took the lead and never looked back. They were totally amazing; talk about kicking butt and taking names! We took a short break, and continued on to Chisapani, which was the small village where we bunked overnight for our final night's stay of the trek. We ate a late lunch, had sodas and beers, and then found some straw mats to catch some of the final rays of sun in the day, snoozing on a hillside terrace. If I had to sleep in a room like that night's accommodations for all three nights of the trek, I might have puked. My entire room/sleeping space was no bigger than 4'x8'x5½' high and the extra two feet beyond the foot of the twin bed was consumed by spider webs and pumpkin/gourd storage. There wasn't a window in the room, so it was very dark and musty, and the small cot took up the entire width of the room, except for a two foot section where the door opened into the room (kept thinking of a tiny room in a nuclear submarine). Remembering the spider adventure from the previous night, I quickly took my flashlight and a straw broom I found on their porch overhang, and fervently made a clean sweep of the room. Doc offered to switch me spots and let me sleep in their room with Deb that night, but I certainly wasn't going to separate them, so I said I could hack it for the night. After everybody changed into warmer clothes and had their baggage secured into their rooms for the night, we all gathered back outside under a straw hut to play Bananagrams. Over the course of this short trek, our porters had become experts in the game, and with each passing night their use of the English language was getting pretty darn proficient (especially with spelling simple words in Bananagrams). We ate a really late supper, and then all hit the hay. When I got back into my room, I brushed my teeth and took my evening dose of Pepto-Bismol (which was a daily regiment for all of us), and then about crapped my pants when I went to put my flashlight down on a ledge near the pillow on my bed and almost set it right into a ½" thick pile of mouse poop. AAAGGGHHH. I threw my toothbrush back into my bathroom necessities pouch, threw that into my luggage, zipped it up, jumped into bed, tightened my hooded sweatshirt around my head, closed my eyes, and convinced myself that I was back at home, with Mabel's chin over my feet and Flossie curled up beside me. My head spun around several more chapters in Kay's book of life, and I drifted off to sleep.

Chapter 19

Tuesday, February 1, 2011

Up early to start our last day of the trek (at that point I was thinking that every village rooster and dog had been up since around 3:00am to serenade us). At some point during the night, I awoke to my stomach being so upset that I seriously did not think I was gonna make it to the squat toilet in time. I wasn't sure if it was something I had eaten at dinner or what, but my stomach was ripped up. So there I was, up and standing vertical in my two foot area that wasn't filled with bed, squash or gourds, throwing on clothes, flexing my sphincter muscle, trying to find my flashlight and toilet paper, dancing back and forth and back and forth telling myself "I can make it, I can make it, I can make it". As I made a mad dash out of my tiny room and into the darkness, I ran smack dab into a *gate* that they had fastened to keep the wild animals out of their living area during the night! Got that opened, and sprinted to the squat toilet. Very close call. Holy shit. Literally. Anyway, up and going that morning with the sun breaking through the fog, and it seemed like every morning on trek, when you walked out of your room and saw the view from where you were at, you had to pinch yourself to really believe what you were living was true. I ate a light breakfast to get my stomach settled, and we all packed our bags, threw more water and snacks into our day packs, and began the descent from Chisapani towards Sundare Danda. This spiraling, dew-covered rock descent was <u>really tricky</u> in the early morning hours, which caused Bill and Doc to both take a slide/tumble on separate occasions, and then later into the morning Felix fell into a barbed-wire fence and scraped up his underarm and sliced his pinky-finger wide open (which would later require a tetanus shot). We cut across some rice fields, made another climb, and then took a quick break at a little village snack shop, where Steve sat down at a table and proceeded to show Krishna how to perform the three-pieces-of-uneven-rope trick. Steve had been promising Krishna that he would teach him how to perform one of his magic tricks at the end of the trek, and the time had come for the card-carrying-Mensa-witty-magician to enlighten his prodigy. I enjoyed witnessing the knowledge exchange between Steve and Krishna, as Steve had finally clued me in on the truth of the blue scarf trick… oh how smart I now felt. It was funny watching Steve explain the rope trip, and to watch Krishna's eyes light up (I could only imagine how Krishna would then incorporate a whole bag of magic tricks into his trek-guide routine). After another long descent, we eventually reached Begnas Tal Lake, where we split up into several canoes and were rowed across the lake to catch the bus transfer back to Pokhara. That had to be one of the most relaxing hours of the entire trek, sitting back in the sun, gliding across a nice quiet lake, thinking about what we had just accomplished over the five days. While hiking with Felix that morning, he and I had quietly discussed whether there was a way to leave our hiking boots in Nepal and donate them to some of these young porters who had been carrying our bags that week (Krishna's nephew spent this whole trek wearing nothing but green high-top canvas gym shoes, which we saw him sewing-to-repair on the very first day). So after the bus ride back to populated civilization, and while waiting at our lunch destination in Pokhara at the Moon Dance restaurant, Felix and I cornered Krishna and asked him if it would be proper for us to offer our hiking boots/shoes to the porters. I told him I especially wanted to leave my boots for his nephew and he said that would be a very generous gift and that he was grateful that I would offer him my boots. I have to admit I got pretty teary-eyed before I did that, because until this Nepal trip, I always thought I wanted my family to bury me in those boots because of their special memories. Hiking with Mike on Camel Back outside of Phoenix and doing the Canyon hike top-to-bottom-to-top all in the same-day adventure with Mike and Young Dendinger, then another trip hiking with Young Dendinger and his girlfriend in Bryce and Zion National Parks (and hiking to the top of Angel's Landing there), and a thousand hikes at Pokagon State Park with family, friends, men in my life, and the dogs. But for some reason, it suddenly meant more to me to leave those boots with that young man who had big ambitions to become a trek guide in Nepal, but without the money to afford hiking boots. So I found Krishna's nephew, and watched his face light up with a smile when I told him I wanted him to give him my boots. I handed him those Vasque Kay-Grand Canyon-Camelback-Bryce-Zion-Pokagon boots with my nice wool socks tucked inside of them, and he gave me a hug. My Christian faith had always led me to share *anonymous gifts of kindness* with a lot of people in my busy days, but that simple act of sharing my boots with a young deserving porter was probably the nicest thing I had done for anybody in a while (and somewhere in heaven, I think my Grandma Cookie smiled down at that one). We all piled back into our transport vehicle after lunch, and we were driven to the Pokhara airport where we said good-bye to Krishna and his nephew. Before we knew it, we were quickly winging our way on Yeti Airlines back towards Kathmandu. I had to admit the Kathmandu airport was starting to look way too familiar, as we landed safety and piled back into a Raya Tours van which delivered us back to our beloved Norbu Linka. We were anxious to take HOT SHOWERS for the first time in way too many days, and that shower was absolutely wonderful, practically indescribable. When I jumped into the shower and washed the shampoo through my hair, I looked down and noticed that the water around my feet was brown from the dirty dust

153

being rinsed off of my hair. Yuck. Five days of hiking with no shower and the joy of trail dust, sweat, and musty gourd smell all being rinsed down a shower at the Norbu Linka (and how many days before I was still able to take a shower in my own bathroom in my own house?). We had a chance to jump on the Internet before dinner, and everybody on Facebook (back in Indiana) was talking about a blizzard that had been predicted in Indiana for the next day or two. The owner of Raya Tours met us in the hotel lobby, and led us on a short 10-minute walk where we were treated to a nice dinner at "Rum Doodles", which was a very cool restaurant frequented by Himalayan trekkers and those who had conquered "the big E." (Mount Everest). Our team wrote messages on a big foot-shaped piece of white thick cardboard which was then nailed to the foot-covered walls; it was great food and a lot of fun to be together for what we deemed our "Last Supper", as we would be separating tomorrow. I loved the atmosphere at that restaurant, and was sad that I would probably never have the chance to frequent that again in my lifetime ☹. On the way back to the hotel, the Raya Tours owner pulled me aside and told me that my bank VISA card had been denied for the trek. What the heck? So I promised that I would make it right with him as soon as I could get in touch with the credit card division of my bank, and he said not a problem, that he would check in with me again in the morning. So I chatted with the Norbu Linka front desk personnel to make sure I knew when the long-distance phone service was working in the hotel (they only had that service available for several hours a day), and since the long distance service was only available from 1:00–5:00am the following day (go figure), my only course of action was to get up during the middle of the night and call my bank. I then left a wake up call for 4:30am, and Linda and I packed and re-organized our bags for our departures tomorrow. After falling asleep hard, I awoke at some God-forsaken hour of the night due to some dogs barking right outside our hotel window, and so I decided to just get up and go to the lobby to see what time it was and possibly call the bank. I grabbed my flashlight, threw on more clothes, quietly grabbed my daypack which held my purse with credit card number, etc., and snuck down the marbled flights of stairs until I hit the icebox lobby level. I proceeded to then wake up the bellboy and the night manager (who were asleep on couches in the lobby), and after several failed attempts at reaching long distance service to call the toll-free phone number on my VISA card, the manager acted like he wasn't going to try any longer. I let out the big "red-headed-bitch sigh" and told him we had to keep trying because I needed to get through to my bank. After several more failed attempts, he looked at *me* as if to say "I give up." Then after giving *him* that dreaded I-am-going-to-kick-your-butt-if-you-don't-listen-to-me-look one more time, he ended up unplugging phone machines, and with phone and computer line cords flying everywhere, he reconfigured everything until we were finally able to get through on the phone line (I gained some real understanding that night of how that bitch-look could get you farther than the English language when necessary). Even though the credit card customer service representative could have very easily been sitting a short flight away from me in a cubicle in India, it was so nice to be able to communicate with someone who spoke fluent English and was extremely helpful and understanding of my frustration. She assured me that my credit card was cleared for use in both Nepal and India, and that if it had been denied she would have had a record of that. So long story short, she said there hadn't been any activity whatsoever on my card since December, so I ended up getting everybody up at 1:00am for nothing, *as there really wasn't a problem with my card after all.* So while I already had both hotel night-shift men awake, they were kind enough to help me get logged back onto the Internet (I figured at that point, while talking between themselves in Nepali, I'm sure they had come to the conclusion they were going to try to appease the red-headed psycho lady with anything she requested of them). I jumped onto Facebook, and got all teary-eyed when I saw that Abby had posted a picture of the amaryllis that one of my fellow Parkview co-workers, Roxanne Varnau, had sent me for Christmas. I had potted it and left it setting on my kitchen countertop before leaving on the trip, and there it was in the picture, on the other side of the world, in full bloom, red and glorious. I was so happy that Mom had gotten the chance to watch it grow and bloom while I was gone! For the next 90 minutes I was instant messaging on Facebook with my sister, Becky, while it was 2:15am Nepal time, 3:15pm Indiana time. How amazing is the Internet that I could send spontaneous messages to my sister, on the other side of the world in a matter of seconds?? At around 3:00am the Internet connection went dead, so I thanked those two guys for helping me with the phone conundrum, and "Little Miss Bitch Was Back until she got through to her bank" took her backpack and flashlight and headed back upstairs to room 108 on the second floor (made me laugh remembering their screwed up room-floor-numbering system). While I was downstairs on the Internet, Linda had gotten up to charge her phone, so in the darkness of room 108 in the middle of the night, there we were, talking about the snow in Indiana, and about whether they would be able to land back in Chicago successfully on Thursday (Marilyn, Felix and Linda were scheduled to fly into Chicago by way of London, so at least they could hopefully get half way home if they couldn't get into Chicago due to the impending blizzard heading towards the Midwest).

Chapter 20

Wednesday, February 2, 2011

After what seemed like a very short night (probably because it WAS), we woke up early and went to the lobby to say our good-byes. It was sad and emotionally-moving to think that a couple of weeks ago I only knew the names of some of these wonderful people on an email distribution list for a Habitat for Humanity trip, and now they had become friends and traveling/trekking buds, and I knew that I would forever miss their camaraderie in my life. Doc, Deb and I were flying on to India for a three-day tour, and the rest of this remaining HFH team were flying back to their respectful parts of the U.S. and Mexico. Doc had arranged for a driver to pick us up at the hotel at 8:00am and take us to "Monkey Temple" in Kathmandu, and so the time came for our departure, we said our good-byes, and away we went. Wow, what an interesting place Monkey Temple was. I loved it. I was so touched by all of the Hindus and Buddhists that were taking the time out of their day to go there and worship, and say prayers for others and themselves. There were COUNTLESS rows of vertically-hung spinning gold and bronze mosaic-etched steel canisters called prayer wheels, and people would walk around them, spinning them with their finger tips as they passed by, chanting. One enclosed room had a huge prayer wheel in it, where you could walk into this domed area and spin the multi-yard-high gold-adorned red cylinder, which had a railing at hip level that everyone pushed along as they walked, which reminded me of a revolving door with everyone shuffling along, praying, chanting, and pushing the outside rim of the cylinder to keep it spinning. There was a monk sitting yoga-style in his maroon-colored robe chanting, and it smelled like they were burning marijuana or some other extremely heavy incense in a huge temple urn (I told Doc and Deb that I hadn't smelled a pot scent quite that strong since attending an outdoor Jimmy Buffet concert near Indianapolis). I was very teary-eyed while there today, spinning all of those rows of prayer wheels, as I kept thinking of my friends, Judi, Pauline, and Carol, and praying that they would stay healthy and strong, and grow old with me as crazy friends. As Deb went around the area walking behind me, she spun prayer wheels and I heard her pray for their church, Marion Mennonite. We continued to wander through the temple grounds, and walked up to a higher part of the temple where those of Hindu faith worshipped. We eventually found a shop where we struck up a deal with a young man and his mother to buy a whole slew of prayer bells for our friends and families. When I told the mother that I was purchasing a prayer bell for my own mom in America, she handed me some prayer flags when we left and she said they were for my mom (Aww, moms are the same, all the way around the world). The monkeys were all over the temple, it was fun to see them sitting together, picking each other's fur, scratching, screeching, etc. Suddenly, coming out of nowhere, one monkey ran up and ripped open the bottom of Deb's plastic bag that contained all of the prayer bells that she had just purchased, and we all screamed and laughed. Even other nearby tourists were laughing at that crazy monkey doing that, as we were sure he was in search of food (that, or he was just really pissed that we were leaving with that many prayer bells). We ended up putting the ripped sack inside my backpack, we found Deb a Coke, and after Doc bartered with a vendor for one last big prayer bell, we found our taxi driver and headed back to the hotel. After entering the icebox lobby, we decided to leave our souvenirs and prayer bells in our luggage before doing some more local shopping over in the Thamel House area as it was warm and sunny outside. I went back to the baggage storage area to get my luggage, where it was being stored prior to our departure for the airport. Absent-mindedly, I forgot there was a glass door *behind* the curtain of the storage room, and I walked full-speed-ahead into the glass door, with my forehead and reverberating body bouncing off of the glass. Deb began to laugh so hard that she about wet herself (and I had to admit, that was the hardest I have laughed at MYSELF in a very long time, too). After rubbing my head for a little bit, we went shopping through the streets of Kathmandu and found maps of the Royal Trek we had just completed, bought playing cards with Nepal pictures on them, and mouse pads for desktop souvenirs, etc. I was anxious to try my credit card to see if we could get it to work this morning, but still no such luck; it came up, "Denied", so we tried Doc's card. When his card had issues also, the shop owners then made a phone call and realized it was the machine, not my card (good thing or I was gonna have to call the credit card folks again and become a real witch this time). We found a place to grab some sandwiches, pizza and pastries, and we sat in the sun and ate lunch at an outdoor table which was heavenly (of course at that point we kind of chuckled at the predicted 13 inches of snow for Indiana that day). In lieu of Deb and I both spotting some jewelry at a previous shopping stop, we then made an attempt to circle back and buy the jewelry, and that ended up being a wild goose chase to another business blocks down the street that hopefully had a credit card machine with a phone line that worked. We ended up telling the merchant to forget it as we had to get back to the hotel to meet the driver to catch our 2:55pm flight to India. After returning to the hotel, we phoned Raya Tours, and this time, after re-checking the numbers on my credit card, the charge went through perfectly (my guess is that they had punched in the numbers wrong the first time). Once arriving at the Kathmandu airport for the umpteenth time on this trip, we made it through the baggage check-in/ticketing area, but then were escorted to a special area to fill out visa extension forms (I teased Doc and Deb that they would do anything to get another stamp in their passport). We were two days beyond the Nepal visa expiration date, which cost us another $36. The plane to Delhi was on-time, and we were winging our way to India before we knew it. As I was glancing out the jet window from my 15E seat at the Annapurna Himalayan mountain range one last time, I got teary-eyed at the thought of leaving Nepal. What an experience this trip had been, and it made me wonder if I would ever see this part of the world again. During the flight I sat in between two men who I assumed were flying to India for work. They appeared to not really know how to use a fork and knife, and I'm pretty sure they were illiterate because neither one appeared to know how to read to fill out the India customs form when the flight attendant passed them out. Doc had pre-arranged for a driver and vehicle to transport us for the next three days that we were scheduled to be in India, but the driver from Ten Travel (the taxi company that Doc had made arrangements with) was not waiting for us at the airport when our jet landed in Delhi as he was scheduled to. Apparently they misunderstood our flight arrival time so they had arrived earlier and then had given up and left the airport… NOT a good thing. After a few moments of frustration (OK, maybe it was more than a *few*), we lucked out and found a very nice young man at a coffee shop within an airport coffee kiosk who was kind enough to help us get on the local Wi-Fi by using his cell phone to text a code to. We found Ten Travel on the Internet and then another very kind porter let us use his cell phone to track them down to guide them to our location within the terminal. The Ten Travel manager eventually arrived to pick us up and when I went back to tip the young man at the coffee shop, he politely tried to not accept my one dollar tip as if that was way too much money. I smiled, handed it to him anyway, and told him to buy something nice for his girlfriend. His face lit up. That was cool, and the other porter denied the tip all together (God was definitely watching

160

out for us, with those two saints at the Delhi airport, for sure). The Ten Travel guy, who spoke very little English and seemed a bit miffed by our frustration with the whole confusing situation, took off leading us to the parking garage towards one of their company's waiting taxis, with our two carts of luggage and us three gringos following behind like lost sheep. We got off of one jammed elevator, walked further, got on to another elevator and the guy proceeded to push the elevator button to take us to the fourth floor. The elevator went up to the fourth floor, but then the doors would not open! He unsuccessfully tried to pry the doors apart, pushed the alarm button, and then he finally started the elevator heading back downwards, which was followed by the elevator lights shutting off, to which he said, "Shit!", which made us Americans, standing in the darkness of the unlit elevator, crack up. We feared we would smash to the first floor, but luckily the elevator came to a stop on the ground floor, the lights came back on, the doors opened, and we were back to where we started from. We couldn't help but laugh as we were nearing tired-and-silly stage, but Mr. Ten Travel seemed to find no humor whatsoever in any of these happenings. So instead of getting off that elevator and onto another elevator that might have been working correctly, he just pushed the 4-button again, the doors closed and away we climbed again, and lo and behold, we got to the fourth floor and guess what, the doors still didn't open!! So he proceeded to pry apart the doors with his hands, and while trying to keep straight faces and not look at each other for fear of bursting out laughing, we wheeled the luggage off, and found our car and driver. The car was small enough that the three of us got into the back seat and we threw two of the bigger bags into the passenger seat in the front (which was on the left side of the car, so it was apparent that the driver sat on the right side of the vehicle in India, also), and away we went. After driving through the streets of Delhi with him chatting away on the phone to another driver that we were meeting up with, we finally found another driver, Ranya, who said he was also one of their Ten

Travel managers, and he helped us switch vehicles and found us a hotel for the night. He was a funny character, and had a much more pleasant personality than the first cat. He told us that in India, he believed three things were needed to be a good driver: Good brakes, a good horn, and good luck. Man, did that guy know what he was talking about, or what?? We decided to stay in Delhi that night instead of trying to get to Agra, India since they told us it would be a five-hour drive. We found a nice hotel, and our room had two twin beds and an extra mattress for the floor, and I volunteered to take the floor spot. Even sleeping on the floor on that mattress was heavenly to me after my "feels-like-concrete-maybe-you'll-be-eaten-by-mice" sleeping experiences on the trek. The movie "Julie/Julia" was on, which had been dubbed in English, and we fell asleep after journaling and giving thanks for finding the driver and this hotel in Delhi.

Chapter 21

Thursday, February 3, 2011
Saw the Taj Mahal!

We were up and going after a 5:30am wake up call so we would be ready to meet our driver at 6:00am for the drive to Agra. To give my eyes a break from my contacts, I had been wearing my glasses the night before while we were watching the Julie/Julia movie, and so when I picked up what I thought were *my* glasses that morning, I had mistakenly packed *Doc's* glasses in my backpack. Just as we were ready to jump into the SUV for the ride to Agra, Doc then discovered that he didn't have his glasses, so Deb sprinted back up to the room to look for them. When I then discovered Doc's glasses in MY backpack, I felt like a dork because I knew I had caused Deb to make a trip back up to the fourth floor to look in the room for them (causing her to use her already-aching knees and leg muscles and blistered feet left sore from our trek). Hey, I *had forewarned them* that I would be their red-headed step-child by the end of this trip! There was an interesting mix of old and new in the surrounding culture as we wove our way out of Delhi towards Agra and the Taj Mahal, with buses, trucks, and covered moped-looking vehicles whizzing beside of us on our journey. Doc and Deb said the roads were so much better than the last time they were here 14 years ago; the area kind of reminded me of a tricked-up Nepal. We began to realize that our new driver for the next three days, Raj, was

163

not very social and didn't seem to speak or understand much of the English language, so we spent the drive to Agra pretty much in silence (Deb took a nap, I updated the trip journal, and Doc rode shotgun up front watching everything going on). Not too far outside of Dehli, we came upon what-appeared-to-be a driver's checkpoint, and Raj pulled the SUV over into a small parking area, took some papers with him, and locked us in as he hopped out. About the time Raj walked away towards another area of the checkpoint, our vehicle was swarmed by local vendors wanting us to buy things, offering to let us take pictures of their monkeys for money, etc. Before we knew it, the "salesman" who had his two monkeys on leashes let his bigger monkey climb up the side of our vehicle. It was clinging to the A-pillar of my window! In my 52 years of life I had never been only an inch away from a living monkey before, and the only thing in between me and the monkey was the glass window. It was pressing its cute little monkey face against the window, blinking his eyes and staring at me! I was trying not to laugh because by then the guy was *yelling* through the closed window for us to take pictures, pay him money, buy anything and everything he was selling, and we were trying to ignore him with look-straight-ahead faces. Finally I got really perturbed at them hawking everything at us, and I hung my fleece jacket from the oh-shit bar above the window, blocking their view of us and they eventually walked away. The monkey was so cute though, and had a belled-collar on… poor monkey. We stopped for breakfast at a roadside café (French toast and mushroom omelets), and the restroom attendant was offended when Deb and I didn't give her a tip after she handed us two quickly-disintegrating paper napkins to wipe our hands with (but we honestly didn't have any Indian rupees yet!). Oh well, rude Americans. The sun came up and turned the day warm, and we continued to make our way towards Agra with zip-zero-nada road signs in English (I continued to be thankful for Raj, even though he wasn't talking a bit). Along the drive I was quite amused when I saw a sign on the back of a big truck that said, "Slow drive. Long life." The way some of these maniacs drove, it's amazing they had lived this long to begin with. We made a pit stop at a McDonald's, which was the first time we had spotted the golden arches on this entire trip! We wound our way through the traffic-packed streets of Agra, and finally found our way to the Taj Mahal parking and entrance area. After we parked, we had to take another smaller vehicle to reach the entrance gate. I was astounded at the first prestigious building we came to, and then the Egli's told me that wasn't even the Taj Mahal; it was just the entrance building! Standing maybe 50 feet tall, the building was constructed out of beautiful sand-colored stone, with marble and gem etchings, just stunning, with big tower belfries at each corner of the building and rows of huge bells running along the sides of the buildings in between the corner towers. At the end of that building was a big domed opening, with steps down to the grounds of the Taj Mahal. That opening was just lit up with the glow of the sun against the white marble of the Taj Mahal; no wonder it was one of the 8 wonders of the world. The fountain pool in front of the Taj Mahal was incredibly long, and it reminded me of the reflection pool in Washington, D.C. between the Lincoln Memorial and the Washington Monument, lined with beautiful mosaic-shaped sections of grass, pierced with tall spiraling shrubs. It was incredible, like nothing I had ever experienced before in my life, and the symmetry and artistic craftsmanship of the Taj Mahal was almost indescribable with words. Only on a grander scale, it still reminded me a lot of the prestige of the Biltmore Estate in Asheville, North Carolina, which I had visited several summers before with my mom and cousins, Bill and Karen Rumpf. We were led around the grounds and through the Taj Mahal by a young man, "Money", who was very knowledgeable with facts and information, and we took lots of pictures that were extraordinary. It was a beautiful, warm day in February (that would have been an oxymoron if describing Indiana) and the sky was a gorgeous blue, so all of the pictures seemed surreal

165

and postcard perfect. I honestly could not believe I was there, at the Taj Mahal, in India! The history of the Taj Mahal was fascinating. The Mughal Emperor Shah Jahan erected the Taj Mahal in memory of his beloved wife, Mumtaz Mahal, whom he first met at the age of 14, and it was love at first sight. Five years later, in 1612, they were married. She died in 1631 after giving birth to their 14th child. Construction on the Taj Mahal started in 1631 and took approximately 22 years to build. An epitome of love, it took the labor of 22,000 humans and 1,000 elephants to complete the project! It was built entirely out of white marble, which was brought in from all over India at the cost of approximately 32 million rupees (approximately $68,000 USD) and now the emperor himself, and his wife, both lie entombed in the mausoleum under the first floor of the Taj Mahal. In order to preserve the sanctity of the temple for future years, they had changed the original entrance and secured wooden planks over the stairs to maintain the marble steps and protect them from the hundreds of thousands of visitors that just flow through, non-stop, during open hours (I read that it is open every day except Friday, when only Muslims are allowed to visit). Everyone going into the temple also had to wear red paper material footies that you were given when you purchased your ticket, which stretched right over your shoes or sandals. If you didn't want to wear the footies, then you had to remove your shoes and place them in storage racks (similar to the racks you would find outside of the children's play area at your local fast food joint) and walk through the temple in your socks or bare feet. So we all donned our little Smurf-looking red slippers over our shoes and sandals (made me giggle when I looked over and thought about Doc doing this whenever he had to gown-up with surgery footies over his shoes in the operating room, and there we were in India with little red slippers on). There were no pictures or videotaping allowed inside of the temple, but our guide was allowed to bring with him a special flashlight so you could see the clarity of the gems when he shined the flashlight against them. We walked through the temple to the back of the property, where the view from the temple balcony was beautiful. Adjacent to this temple and across the river, was the site where, as legend has it, the king's son wanted to build a second Taj Mahal out of black marble; but as history revealed, that project never came to fruition. After taking countless pictures, we left the grounds of the Taj Mahal and Money took us to several jewelry/marble shops within Agra, so that we could see the gems found in India that were used in making the temple. After several stops without any purchases to the apparent chagrin of Money (we surmised he possibly would have gotten a kickback from any souvenirs we bought), we found a restaurant with outdoor tables under umbrellas to eat lunch and enjoy the last few remaining hours of sunshine before we had to head back to snowy Indiana, three days away. After lunch we said goodbye to Money, and Raj headed our SUV out of Agra towards Fatehpur Sikri. Shortly after leaving the restaurant, we got caught in a HUMONGOUS traffic jam, which ended up being pure entertainment for us (Raj might have been frustrated, but us three Americans thought it was a hoot). We sat for 45 minutes in stopped traffic right within a small village shopping area, with everything imaginable passing our vehicle, staring at us light-skinned foreigners inside. We snapped pictures galore through the windows, and finally we were able to pass and get around the street paving crew and the big steamlike-but-steamless roller that was causing the traffic jam in the first place. About an hour out of town, we came to a human roadblock and our SUV was forced off the road by some men who demanded that our driver leave the vehicle and come with them to talk (that became the one and only time I felt even somewhat scared on the entire trip outside of the United States). When Raj left the vehicle, he locked us inside and walked back to talk to a group of men. One of the men then returned to our vehicle, and walked up to Doc's window and he kept demanding (through the glass) that Doc roll down the window. Of course with Deb and I continually saying, "Don't roll down the window!", Doc knew better too, and kept telling the demanding-man that he could hear him through the window, that he was not going to roll down the window. Our take on the situation was that they were the local tour guides, and were demanding that they be allowed to take us on to Fatehpur Sikr. It did occur to me that no one on the entire planet had any idea where we were at that moment… it would have been like a "48-Hours Mystery" episode, if we had turned up missing. We turned around to look for Raj, who was walking back towards our vehicle continually shaking his head, as if to say no. He was hounded the whole walk back to our vehicle by the apparent head honcho of the roadblock gang, who was dogging him the entire way. Eventually Raj got in the SUV and he never did explain in English what the situation was about; he just kept shaking his head. Whoa. Deb and I kind of sat back in our seats and with an eye-roll, let out a sigh of relief as we pulled away and were on the road again. Fatehpur Sikri is a complex of red sandstone monuments and temples built during the second half of the 16th century by the Emperor Akbar. It was the capital of the Mughal Empire for only about ten years, until they ran out of a water supply to sustain the growing population and had to move the capital. When we arrived at the entrance to Fatehpur Sikri, we left Raj at the SUV, and started to walk towards the park gates. When we realized we only had about 30 minutes to tour before they closed the gates, we decided to pass on entering, but were then surrounded by hawkers who didn't comprehend the word, "no". We proceeded to push by them to look for a restroom, and when we found it, we ended up passing on that, too, as there was a charge to pee! So we quickly hopped back into our vehicle and took off for Jaipur, our destination for that evening. When Raj stopped and got out to pay a road tax several miles down the road, Doc rolled down his window and bought several oranges from a roadside orange-hawker ☺. They were good, and we gave one to Raj when he returned to the SUV too. The drive from there to Jaipur ended up being a three-hour tour for Skipper, Ginger, and Marianne, so we had lots of time to talk, nap, and journal on the way. Money (our tour guide back in Agra) had called ahead to get us a room at the Sheraton, but when we arrived in Jaipur after dark, we found we were at the wrong Jaipur Sheraton, but lucked out because the Four Points Sheraton did have a room available and it was 7000 rps instead of 12000 rps, so we were living large (we had gone from mice-status in Biratnagar to five-star in Jaipur!). We got on the elevator to go to the fourth floor (to room 4411), and laughed when we had to push the "4" button, remembering that last time we did that in the Delhi airport we had gotten stuck in an elevator with no lights! It felt like heaven when we opened the room door. It was a classy hotel room with white cushy down-filled bedspreads with a view overlooking the city and the swimming pool area. The glass shower jutted out into the living room and had internal shower blinds that you pulled down so everybody in the room wouldn't see you showering. Deb took a funny picture through the glass wall of me and Doc in the shower with our clothes on! We went down to the hotel restaurant and had nice meals; John had fish, Deb had chicken Parmesan, and I had a chicken breast sandwich. YUM. After dinner we checked the Internet, found they had nine inches of snow at home, sent some emails, then we all showered one by one (with screens lowered of course!) and hit the sack after Doc gave me a nice pill to settle my "Kathmandu crud" cough for the night so we could all sleep.

Chapter 22

Friday, February 4, 2011
Deb's birthday! Saw a live tiger!

Up with a 6:00am wake up call so we could eat at the free breakfast buffet, which was really nice... eggs, pancakes (yes, with maple syrup!), muffins, omelets, fresh fruit and varieties of juice (watermelon juice!), and baked goodies. Our driver and vehicle were outside the lobby waiting for us when we finished breakfast, and we were pretty sure Raj had slept in the vehicle in a park last night (his English was never understandable and he didn't seem to comprehend a lot of what we asked him). We left Jaipur, and headed towards the lion preserve at Ranthambhor National Park. *However,* somewhere along the way Raj took a wrong turn (insert Gilligan Island theme song here... "The ocean started getting rough, the tiny ship was lost, if not for the courage of the fearless crew the Minnow would be lost, the Minnow would be lost"). We didn't catch the wrong turn since you couldn't read a single freakin' road sign (in English), and with Raj apparently not knowing the best route, we therefore unknowingly continued in the wrong direction. We started heading west towards Ajmer and wound our way through one-lane roads and small villages for over an hour off-course, ended up heading back east at Tonk, and eventually made our way over to the national park. *If you had a notion to let it be frustrating,* everything could have been frustrating there... the roads weren't marked well and our driver never seemed too confident about whether he knew where he was going. He never talked much, but we all got the impression that he might have just been a taxi driver, and that driving folks around for three days outside of the Delhi city limits was probably way outside of his normal routine. The three of us remained very thankful that we had Raj transporting us, because if we had been trying to navigate our way through India on our own in a rental car, we would have been so screwed. All of the road signs there were written in Sanskrit, and it was rare to see English anywhere, so we rarely had a clue on where to turn or how far ahead things were. So long story short, even though we ended up being way off course, we had a wonderful morning just riding along and gawking out the windows. In one village, within one small grass yard, I saw this combination of animals: 1 camel, 1 pig, 1 dog and 2 goats. Now how many yards in America would have contained that?? I found the camels very intriguing, most of them were adorned with colorful designs painted or branded on their fur (as if their owner wanted to upgrade their ride), and their eyes and nostrils were huge. We finally found our way to the tiger preserve, and drove through the front of the park and saw samba deer and some other beautiful, unusual birds, but then figured out we had to go back into the village area to buy the tickets and arrange for transportation through the park (here's the shocker: there weren't legible signs or instructions on where/when/how/whom to buy the tiger tour tickets from – no shit Sherlock). We found a government-owned hotel and the owner assisted us in making accommodations for the tour (with a small fee for himself, of course), and we grabbed some chicken sandwiches, fries and Cokes in his restaurant (not up to American par, but good all the same). We sat in the shade outside of the hotel under a big tree until the tiger tour folks came to pick us up around 1:45pm for the tour (the cost of touring the tiger conversation area was a whopping 200 Indian rps, or the equivalent of $4 USD). We hopped upon an open-top jeep/bus with about 21 other people, some were on the bus already and others we stopped and picked up at a really cool resort, Alsisar. Everyone entering the tiger preserve had to fill out liability forms and hand them to the guide (getting eaten by a tiger might have topped my excitement-list for 2011), who then turned them in at a checkpoint as we entered the park. A uniformed park ranger came out and jumped aboard our jeep, officially dressed with an olive beret atop his head, and he proceeded to check our names against a manifest list. We also had to show him our passports to verify that we were the person who had purchased a ticket and that we were on the bus (the security here seemed tighter than at the Kathmandu airport; was there a national threat against their tigers or something??). We took the same road into the park that we drove on that same morning, but turned down a different side road to get back into tiger territory. There were other buses and jeeps in the park at the same time besides the one we were riding in, and you drove around through different regions of the park, all in search of a glimpse of even one of the 32 adult and 14 tiger cubs that roamed around and lived within these 151 square miles. The land was originally established as a game sanctuary by the government of India in 1955, and was then declared a tiger preserve in 1973. It became a national park in 1984, and even more land was set aside and added to the park in 1991. We saw many deer, and countless species of birds and mongoose, and Deb and John were laughing on the play of words with mongoose… when you're talking about mongoose, are there men-goose and lady-goose and if there's more than one, would that be mongeese or mongooses? Ha-ha. The park was also known for leopards, wild boar, samba deer, hyena, and sloth bear, but we only saw the samba deer (and lots of them). It had to be about 80 degrees that day, and it was so nice and warm and sunny riding around in that open-top jeep… what a great day to be alive. Along the way we kept seeing these birds which we later identified as a treepie; they were brownish black on the back of their body with a golden chest, with extremely long tail feathers. They were so pretty. While we were stopped along one of the paths taking pictures of deer, all of a sudden one of those treepie birds flew down and sat on the roll bar of the jeep, right beside this lady's head. The guide explained that we didn't need to be frightened, because those birds were very friendly and that they liked sweets. We continued on through the park, eyes going every which way, trying to spot anything tiger-like moving in the bush. We stopped and took a 15-minute break along the way, and Doc took an Oreo cookie out of his backpack, and held it up, and I could have sworn that I overheard all of those treepie-long-tailed-sweet-hankering birds sitting around us in the trees yell out, "Game on!" They began to swoop down from everywhere, and so I got out my trail mix too, and started dumping it in everybody's hands, and we took so many cool pictures of those treepies, eating right out of everyone's hands! One bird had his little feet/claws wrapped around my thumb as a perch, just chomping down on the trail mix in my palm! I know for sure that I was much more in awe at that point than the birds were, they were just happy to find some free grub! We took off driving again, and had come to a stop amidst a large grove of trees taking pictures of a family of monkeys up in the tree tops surrounded by a herd of deer underneath them. Suddenly all of the animals started sending out warning calls. The monkeys were going nuts, and the deers' ears were alert, with their tails standing straight up. Our guide quickly grabbed some binoculars from a guy sitting near the front of our bus, and started searching through the brush in the horizon. There were some other jeeps around ours, and suddenly everybody started yelling and our guide told everybody to sit down and hang on, and you could tell that the hunt was on, it was so exciting! We went up over a small ridge and there she was. A large, beautiful tigress. When we first spotted her, she was drinking out of a small stream deep in a wooded area and you could only get an occasional glimpse of her, but she eventually began to walk towards us, up a small incline through a brushy area. Everybody was silently going *nuts,* snapping pictures like mad; you could hear the gentle sounds of shutter frames clicking away in non-stop rhythm. Everyone was standing up on seats, crawling up onto the roll bars, trying to get a really good picture. Little by little that stealth majestic creature made her way up the small incline, and walked right in front of all of the Jeeps. She cruised by so effortlessly, so slow, so powerful, so strong, so sure of herself, as if there weren't a whole herd of nuts-o people standing on buses and jeeps snapping her every move in a hundred simultaneous picture frames. *She never even turned her head our way.* She nonchalantly continued walking right into the woods on the other side of the road, and everybody was so thrilled that we had beaten the odds and were lucky enough to see a REAL tiger, in her own habitat, that close, with nothing in between us and a tiger but thin air. The minute she was out of sight, everybody was sitting back down in their seats (with laughter and a lot of whopping it up and O.M.G.'s filling the air), messing with their cameras to flow back through their pictures on their camera cards to see who got a really good picture of her. I cracked up as I then realized that in my awe of seeing the tigress in real-life without looking through the camera lens, I didn't get ONE PICTURE of her saved on my camera, but at least I will always have her memory. My pictures contained the heads, backsides and butts of everybody in front of me – so much for being a short person! The guide said that particular tigress was 16-years old, and told us her name (at which point Deb and I looked at each other and said he was feeding us all a line of bull), and reported that she was the only tiger seen in the preserve that day (OK, I might have believed that part of his schpeel). We continued to see a lot of other animals on the way out of the park, but no more tigers! It was so wonderful that not only did Deb get to see a real live tiger on her birthday, but so did another lady from Canada… it was her birthday, too, and she was on the same bus we were! What were the odds of that??? Two birthdays and one tiger! We exited the tour bus where they had picked us up;

we met Raj and found our vehicle, and headed back towards Jaipur. It took us almost three hours to make that drive back, the roads were horrible, sometimes down to one lane, with traffic coming at us head-on and swerving around vehicles in front of us, with low lights or no lights (camels, etc.). When we finally arrived back to the Four Points Sheraton, we were all still hungry, so we ordered room service while Deb took a quick shower, and Doc and I ran downstairs to check the Internet. Back in Indiana, Ab was sick with a sore throat and everybody was still Facebooking about the mega inches of snow that had fallen since I left Auburn. Room service came, and Deb had a fruit plate and a walnut brownie with double ice cream for her birthday dinner! Doc caught up on his journal, we all re-organized our bags for tomorrow's flight towards home, and we hit the hay with great memories of a tigress rolling through our memories!

Chapter 23

Saturday, February 5, 2011
Got sunburned while riding an elephant!

We slept in until 7:30am, got up and showered and finalized our packing before grabbing a very filling breakfast in the hotel prior to heading to Amber Fort. We checked the Internet to see whether Kevin Miller (who had kindly agreed to pick us up at the Chicago airport) had responded to our earlier message about whether the snow would prohibit him from getting to the Windy City to pick us up. He replied that we were probably going to be shocked to come back to three feet of snow on my car, and that Doc's son (J.J.) was going to try to get the tractor out of the Egli garage and plow out their driveway. Seriously, after being in 70–80 degree heat each afternoon, the thought of going back to snow was going to take an attitude adjustment! Raj had brought a local guide with him when he picked us up that morning, someone who knew the area and a little more about the fort, since Raj didn't seem to be too knowledgeable about the city of Jaipur. With an additional person in our vehicle, that meant that the three of us gringos would have to sit in the middle two seats of the SUV (because our luggage took up the rear section). It ended up working out OK, as Deb and I squished together and put both of our butts on her seat behind the driver on the right side of the vehicle, with Doc riding in the seat behind the passenger. After leaving the hotel, we began to drive through several districts of Jaipur heading towards Amber Fort, and all of a sudden the traffic in front of us came to a screeching halt. Raj slammed on the breaks and slightly rear-ended the vehicle in front of us, and I fell forward towards the opening between the front seats (...Remember... no seat, yet alone a seat belt, in the back seat for my butt). Luckily I caught myself on the back of the driver's seat before flying forward even more, and Raj got out and checked for damage. There wasn't any damage to either vehicle, and we proceeded on our way (thank God for flexible foreign SUV bumpers). The fort in the distance was beautiful, and to get to the fort entrance, we chose to ride up the stone pathway to the fort on an *elephant*, which was TOTALLY AMAZING. Doc and Deb went first. You had to step off of a platform and climb onto a flat box which was fastened to the elephant's back like a saddle, and then a steel bar was swung across your lap and fastened you in, just like a carnival ride at the Auburn Free Fall Fair! As their elephant proceeded on up the hill, another elephant moved towards the platform, and his big, gray, leather-like ear was flapping against my feet on the platform. Oh my gosh, right there was a real elephant and its ear was brushing my feet! It was then my turn to step off of the platform and climb aboard, and so our tour guide climbed aboard the elephant with me and away we went! The elephants were such unique, amazing creatures, and I had never been this close to an elephant before in my life (although I did have a flashback to taking Alex to the circus at the Fort Wayne Coliseum and watching an elephant fill up a 20-gallon wooden circus barrel with urine in no time flat). The elephant's huge ears were flapping back and forth as if he was happy, and I couldn't wipe the smile off of my face. I wanted to *scream out loud,* "O.M.G., look at the elephant's ears!" I couldn't believe how high off the ground we were, and how the elephant swayed from side to side while he lumbered along. My elephant seemed slower than the rest of the elephants while making this long, slight-incline trek towards the fort, and I remember thinking I was kind of glad he was hokey-pokey because it made the ride last a long time! When I asked, the elephant owner said in broken English that his elephant was 25-years old (of course if he had been 50-years old would I have known the difference??). With my elephant plodding slowly along, an elephant-traffic-logjam ensued in the flow on the stone-laid pathway leading up to the top of the fort. There had to be 40 elephants making the trek, some going up carrying riders, and some coming back down empty. My face was practically cracking from smiling so hard. I took lots of pictures; it was just unbelievable to me that I was experiencing this! Some elephants had their trunks painted in bright beautiful colors to make them showy with neon pink, yellow, and aqua colors. Every once in a while my elephant would blow air/snot out of his trunk and it would spray off of the flat stone walkway and the surrounding walls and then I could feel it hit me, which made me laugh thinking, "I'm in India, getting sunburned while riding an elephant, and now I'm feeling elephant snot! Wow!" I couldn't contain my laughter, and I thought of my father-in-law, Joe Donaldson, the whole way up the steady climb to the fort, and how much he would have been thrilled by riding an elephant like that. The Egli's were at the top long before *my* newly adopted elephant got up there – what a sight it was to walk through the gateway of that huge fort atop an elephant! The fort was amazing, built in the early 1600's out of sandstone, comprised of incredible architectural talent and craftsmanship, and yet built long before our modern tools and engineering prowess existed. Our guide kept wanting to push us (we got the feeling that he had other places/shops in Jaipur he wanted us to "experience"), so Doc finally told him in a frank-but-nice-way that THIS was what we came here to see, we didn't care about seeing anything else that day, and that we were going to pay him to go sit down and wait for us. The guide seemed a little unsure of that new concept, but he accepted it and walked away to go sit down and patiently wait for us. We were then able to take our time, wandering throughout the fort unguided, and explored rooms, hallways and crevices on our own. It was great, and we took so many beautiful pictures while soaking in the architecture and shadows, shapes, textures; it was picture paradise. As soon as we exited, we were hit up by all of the photograph hawkers who had taken our elephant-ride pictures - pretty amazing how quickly they were able to scan through all of their printed pictures and then spot us in the crowd of exiting tourists, probably by the clothing we had on, our hair color, my backpack, etc. Nothing like three gringos standing out amidst thousands of Indians and Chinese. Doc did a good job of negotiating with them, and he finally bartered them down to purchase four 5"x7" pictures for 150 rps (little under $4 USD). Our guide then hit us with a newly angled sales pitch and said that it was "compulsory" that he take us to a marble factory (that might have been the final straw for the tour-guide relationship and we were "long out of nice" by then). Doc put his foot down and said, nope, he wasn't gonna take us to any marble factory, that we just wanted to head to Delhi to the airport. Raj did a good job of backing down this new tour guide, who by then was probably frustrated with our lack of cooperation in dropping more money into his local economy. We weren't too far outside of the fort when Mr.-Let-me-be-your-tour-guide-and-see-how-quickly-I-can-piss-you-off said that he was getting off there, and so he hopped out of our vehicle, Doc handed him a tip, and we said good-bye (so much for the compulsory marble factory visit!). Raj pointed our vehicle towards Delhi and we stopped to take some pictures of elephants and camels along the road, and also snapped shots of a beautiful castle that appeared to be built on an island right in the middle of a lake in Jaipur. During this entire trip, Deb had attempted to get a picture of a Massey Ferguson tractor, and she finally spotted one as we were stopped in traffic that afternoon on the ride out of Jaipur! She had Doc's borrowed camera open to take the picture, and as we began to move through traffic the camera wasn't focusing quickly enough, and she turned around and screwed up her words when in disgust at missing the picture she said, "I couldn't get a pictor of that

Massey Ferguson tracture!" Then, as we were all cracking up at her getting her words all twisted up, she proclaimed, "And now my battery's dead!" At this point in our long journey thru Nepal and now India, I felt like I was becoming a little brain-dead myself, as it was hard to even remember what day it was. It seemed like it had been months since I left Auburn, or had worked a day at Parkview, and it even seemed like it had been weeks since we had said goodbye to our Habitat friends in Kathmandu and headed to India. As extraordinary as this trip had been, I was equally also ready to go home. I had never been away for three weeks, and with each passing day, my heart grew heavier for home. I missed my family and my dogs, I missed picking up the phone and talking with my kids, or hearing Baylie laugh or seeing Gage smile at his grandma. I hadn't heard their voices in over 22 days, and that physically made my heart ache when I paused from journaling to count those days on my fingers. Besides holidays, I would now have to work almost every single day for an entire year because of the vacation days this trip had cost me, but at that moment, that meant absolutely nothing to me. Nothing. The even funnier part of realizing that, was before taking this trip, if someone had asked me to donate my saved weeks of earned Parkview vacation time to a needy co-worker, I probably would have selfishly thought about the family time that I would have sacrificed to do that, and I would have said no. Shame on me. This trip not only enlightened me to two different colored countries on the floating globe on my Parkview office desk, but now I knew that one of my business acquaintances, Karen Rak was right. She forewarned me one day that I would, in the end, ultimately refer to this trip as "a journey", because it would end up affecting me physically, mentally, and spiritually. All of her words and those thoughts spun through my head, and I smiled because I knew Karen was spot-on. I was heading home a different Kay than when I had left. For the past three weeks I had witnessed more poverty than I could have ever imagined possible, and that, in itself, would come to scar my heart for a long time. Commonplace on this portion of the globe seemed to be a lack of what I could have ever imagined for proper food, clothing, and shelter, and yet no one that I met on this journey seemed upset, frustrated, worried, or sad about it. They re-used and functioned in ways I couldn't comprehend, and even though I had been in this culture for three weeks now, wherever we drove, I found myself staring out the window as the world was whizzing by and I continued to feel untapped emotions that hadn't surfaced before. I now had 1,297 pictures on my current camera card and a million more memories that were etched on my heart. Even with the long flight home from India still lying ahead of us, I felt like God had brought me to yet another plateau in my life, with another few pieces of the puzzle of my life now uniquely snapped into place. I had been putting off writing a book for years, because I never knew what to write about. Oh that little trickster Bob Pruitt, he had been right all along; it was there inside of me, just waiting to pour out. The trip back towards Delhi went quickly, and Raj (along with his trusty front-left-seat-sidekick, Doc) did a great job of weaving in and out of traffic while Deb and I tried our best to stay awake during the warm, mid-afternoon drive. We found a McDonald's along the way, what a treat, and I changed out of my elephant-riding clothes and into my airport clothes, which was a bit tricky considering they had just mopped the bathroom floor (but after countless days of improving my squat pot technique, changing clothes while standing on that wet floor was a piece of cake). We bought Raj a sandwich too, so we all had McChicken sandwiches, fries and Diet Cokes! It was heavenly! The arteries were re-clogging already! We got to the airport in great time, gave Raj our tip money for escorting us for the past three days, and *then* the leaving-India-pre-flight conundrum began. Apparently there was some confusion about Ten Travel not getting the Egli's credit card information (which he had previously sent to them in an email), and so Raj wasn't going to let us leave the airport without him writing down a credit card number to charge the tour to, and we weren't too keen with giving him our credit card number on a piece of paper! Eventually Doc got it all straightened out by reading his credit card info to the Ten Travel office folks over the phone, and we checked our bags for the flight from Delhi to Abu Dhabi. We proceeded to plop down in some soft airport chairs (yet another trip oxymoron?) and got on the airport Wi-Fi to find a Chicago weather report for our Sunday arrival there. Deb did a little birthday shopping, and found a gorgeous butterfly and lily scarf for herself and some others scarves for gifts. It was so cute when she was modeling her new scarf and said, "On this trip I didn't buy significant jewelry, but I did buy significant scarves." Ha-ha. Deb had been sporting two nasty foot blisters since the trekking adventure, so she grabbed a free ride down to Gate #7 aboard the airport golf cart shuttle service, and Doc and I walked to the gate and reminisced about the HFH build and how much fun we had working with everybody. Then a miracle happened (and since it was 10:00pm India time, I thought maybe I was already asleep and just having a good dream). As we proceeded through the boarding line for the Abu Dhabi flight, the young flight attendant at the ticket counter scanned my boarding pass, and wanted me to verify that there were three people in our party. I said yes, and he drew a line through seat 12A on my boarding pass, changed it to seat 4C, and told me that he was moving the three of us to Business Class. We all about crapped! Woo-hoo! What a fun time, as we spent the next three-hour flight from Delhi to Abu Dhabi living l-a-r-g-e. We were like three kids in a candy shop when we plopped down into those cushy, extra-roomy business class seats (my guess is that would be the one and only First Class flying experience of my lifetime). We looked in every compartment, checked out the seat features and all the amenities, etc., and realized how the people that usually sit in these seats must travel (I doubted there were squat pots or mice on their vacation adventure lists). I took the wooden hanger out of the storage pocket on the seat in front of me, and said to Deb, "Ma'am, may I hang up your camouflage coat for you?" We began to look at the dinner menu, and I leaned across the aisle and asked Deb, "Do you think if I asked the flight attendant if I could take this menu home for a souvenir, that it would mark me as a redneck?" I think it might have been a combination of realizing what a fantastic trip this had been, and having a lot of fun just relaxing with the thought we were heading home, but we all had the sillies. At one point I glanced over at them, and Doc was toasting me with his glass of white wine, with his pinky finger extended into the air to exude class. It was hilarious! The meal was great, we had many choices of things to eat and drink, and I ended up choosing the Caesar salad, tomato basil soup, prawns in hot garlic sauce served with egg fried rice and stir-fried vegetables, various rolls and garlic toast, and key lime pie for dessert. Yum. After the meal, when they brought us hot washcloths to cleanse our hands, I had a good laugh when Deb put her hot washcloth across her face, and said to me, "Facial". We decided then and there that upon arrival, we would go check to see if there was any way that we could use our ticket stubs to gain entrance into the first class lounge at the Abu Dhabi airport so we could be a little more comfortable during the next 11-hour layover. As the day quickly turned into night, I glanced across the aisle, and Deb was already taking a post-glasses-of-champagne nap, while Doc was writing in his journal, and I was typing like a mad woman on the Notebook. I looked up at the digital flight information on the monitor screens hanging above the seats and noticed that we were cruising at 459 mph, and that it was –49 degrees C outside. It reflected that we were flying over the Gulf of Oman at about 33,959 feet (slightly different flight from the spring break trip where I flew in a private small six-seat plane to Florida and came home with a tramp-stamp tattoo on my lower back). At the point in the flight where the indicator said we had less than an hour left in the flight (296 miles to go), I was trying so hard to stay awake and flip my body back onto Indiana time, as I had to be back to work on Monday morning. That meant that I was going to try to stay awake during the upcoming layover, and then take some naps and watch movies during the long flight from Abu Dhabi to Chicago. We landed in Abu Dhabi around midnight, and then prepared ourselves for the 11-hour layover. We found an empty horizontal chair and tried to camp out to grab three of those horizontal chairs in a row to rest in during the long night ahead, but then Doc searched around and found us a quieter gate in another area of the airport that had carpet on the floors. We grabbed our carry-on bags and moved over closer into that area, which was also the location of the gate we would be departing from the next morning. I spent the night checking emails, reading, and doing a little airport shopping (found some nice new Prada perfume, etc.). Around 5:00am while I was IM'ing my sister Becky (in Indiana), the Buddhist chants were played over the loud speaker throughout the entire airport, which even stirred sleeping Doc! Around 5:30am Doc officially woke up, and we all took the elevator with our cart filled with luggage up to the second floor airport fast food court where we had Burger King Whoppers, fries, and onion rings! And diet Cokes with ICE! Heavenly! We came back downstairs and did some shopping (I finally bought my camel, Humphrey, that I ogled over the first time we flew through Abu Dhabi, and two smaller camels for Baylie and Gage), checked Facebook, and got ready to board the plane for our 10:25am Etihad Airlines westbound flight to Chicago. This was going to be the first day in over three weeks that we seemed to be back on the same day with our loved ones back home.

Chapter 24

Sunday, February 6, 2011

The flight home was an extremely LONG one – a 16-hour non-stop, travel-through-time warp, like an Abu Dhabi to Chicago kind of bad dream, with Doc feeling pretty nauseous most of the flight. I watched a couple of movies, read, ate two meals, and got up and moved around the airplane aisles on occasion just to keep my lower legs and feet from swelling. At one point the guy in the seat next to me spilled his glass of water down the side of my jeans, soaking my foot, so I took off my sock and spread it out over my seat table to dry. Would somebody *please* explain to me why I always get seated next to people who shake or spill stuff? We landed in Chicago on time, and after passing through customs and gathering our luggage at the carousel (which took forever – man, there were A LOT of people on that big jumbo jet), we spotted the friendly face of Kevin Miller waiting to pick us up and drive us back to Topeka. Kevin had driven to Chicago the previous evening, in case the snow had piled up and he couldn't drive over on the toll road from Indiana on Sunday). I had made arrangements to include Kevin on a surprise for the Egli's, as I wanted to give Doc and Deb a nice wall hanging/picture for helping me with the entire trip planning/flights/scheduling/traveling tips, etc. So before we left Topeka three weeks prior, I had left the wall hanging with Tom and Morag Miller at the Topeka Pharmacy, and Kevin stopped there after he was done teaching school for the day at Westview, and picked it up to keep it in the Egli Tahoe while we were gone so I could give it to them when we landed in Chicago. I knew I could have never made parts of this trip without their knowledge and guidance, and the kindness of their invitation to visit India with them was something I will always treasure. The toll road drive from Chicago heading east towards Indiana wasn't bad at all; the majority of the snowfall had passed through during the night, so the roads had been pretty much cleared off by that afternoon. Doc still wasn't feeling up to par, so he slept most of the way home while Kevin briefed us on what had happened in northeast Indiana in the past three weeks while we had been gone. We dropped Kevin off at his house in Shipshewana and continued on to Egli's home in Topeka, where even with a running start, we were barely able to get up the steep drive to their house due to some major ice under all of that snow. I was so grateful that Doc and Deb helped me shovel out and clean off my car, even though I knew for a fact that Doc pretty much felt like hell-warmed-over at that point. We threw my luggage in my car, gave each other a hug, and I took off down the hill and headed towards Auburn (good thing Doc had the foresight three weeks ago to park my car in the downhill direction!). I had a hard time staying awake on the 40-minute drive from their house to my house in Auburn through the snow, and the drive seemed to take forever (it was SO odd to be in *my* car, *driving* again). But heading down the quiet Auburn streets, when I rounded the small curve and eventually spotted my little white house with sand-colored shutters in the glow of the street light, it sure was a welcoming sight. And as I pulled into my driveway, there was my loving mom, Flossie and Mabel, and Abby and Jason, all looking out my living room window, waiting for me to come *home.* Boy, if that wasn't enough to bring tears to my eyes. I'm not sure the dogs even remembered who I was at first; they definitely were happy and content to have Grandma fulfilling their every need in life while I was gone. After some hugs, we spent the next several hours talking and chatting, looking at the souvenirs in my bags and throwing clothes into the washer, before I finally hit the hay around 1:45am. The alarm then went off at 5:45am; talk about getting shocked back to reality. What an awesome mom I have. She made breakfast for us while I showered, dried my hair, put in my contacts, then put on make-up and slapped on jewelry, a business suit and high heels. I warmed up the car since it was 28 degrees, downed the Mom-made breakfast and slipped back into the regular weekday routine of my previous life, still unsure of who this new Kay was and how to comprehend the things that she had just experienced in life. What an adventure of a lifetime, one I will certainly never forget. Nepal – Habitat for Humanity – Himalayan trek – India. Just an unbelievable journey on borrowed time.

Epilogue

Beginning that very first day back on U.S. soil, I knew the simplest things in my life would never be taken for granted again. After a couple of nights of sleeping back in my own soft bed with Flossie and Mabel, and being able to brush my teeth with tap water or use the restroom without first having to pause to think about where my roll of toilet paper was, my life slowly returned to its normal, but-somewhat-insane, routine. I was sooooo thankful for my Parkview co-workers who were anxious to see me and hear about my trip. They were equally as compassionate and helpful to let me ease back into reality on a gentle glide, allowing me to catch up on hundreds of unread emails and remember passwords and responsibilities that I had been void of during my three weeks away. I was SO happy to see my children and my grandchildren, and the sight of Baylie and little Gage wearing their Nepali woven hats that I brought home for them, brought tears to my eyes. Mom stayed at my house for a couple of days after I was home, just to help me get back into the swing of things and slowly wean Flossie and Mabel off of the pleasure of having Grandma tend to their every need 24/7. The swelling in my ankles and calves from mountain altitudes and the lack of circulation during the 16-hour flight home eventually left my body, and the Kathmandu coughing crud dissipated from my lungs after several evenings of breathing some good Hoosier air while walking the dogs in the snow. I soon returned to my 5:00am spinner-bike routine which helped me get back into the correct time zone and insync with my pre-trip daily schedule, and with the fabulous talents of our Parkview Corporate

Office cafeteria chefs, Ryan Eckert and Debbie Fleck, their scrumptious lunch-time meals quickly had my after-work-jeans fitting my body again (without sliding off of my hips like they did after the Nepal work-site workout and the Himalayan weight-loss trekking adventure). Going back to the grocery store, for the first time after returning home, was a reminder of the food we have in abundance and readily available in my Indiana world. When I placed a cored pineapple in my shopping cart and noticed the container read "grown in Costa Rica", and the blueberry container was stamped "grown in Chile", I paused and wondered what it was like in those countries (my world had now been expanded in unimaginable ways). My first Saturday morning after returning home, alone in my house with Floss and Mabel, was a treasured one. After adjusting all week to being back on American time and returning to a hurried work pace, I woke up, alarm-clock free, to Mabel's muzzle softly brushing my cheek and little Flossie walking up on top of my chest to stretch and say good morning. The simple pleasure of letting them out for their morning romp in my snowy backyard and watching them run around like maniacs with snow flying from their heels, brought such laughter to my soul. After brushing the snow off of their feet (and the we-need-a-biscuit routine that always follows each time they come back into the house), I proceeded to mix up some pancakes by scratch, enjoying the simplicity of breaking the eggs, measuring the oil and mixing up the batter while listening to the Pandora Radio-Chris Tomlin playlist on my Droid. As I slowly dropped fresh blueberries into each pancake and watched them bubble up in the skillet, I was overcome with praise and thanksgiving for my humble life in a small snowy city in northeast Indiana, almost 8,000 miles away from little Dashrath and his family outside of Biratnagar, Nepal. For weeks after returning home, my nightly dreams were filled with the people that I had become attached to in Nepal. One night I dreamed I was canoeing down a stream with little Babita in my canoe, and I saw her dark-skinned face with its bright eyes and beautiful smile as if I were still two feet from her, slapping mud onto the walls of her new home. The canoe in front of us in the dream contained Rajesh (HFH coordinator) and Jac Price, PLH Board Chairman. Their canoe flipped over, and I dove into the water to save Jac, but first had to unbuckle his seat belt (in a canoe??), which I then realized was the same seatbelt that I had fastened each day while riding in Raj's vehicle through India. I woke up from the dream breathing heavily, reached out for the comforting touch of Flossie's soft fur, tucked my feet back under Mabel and fell right back to sleep. None of that dream made any sense, but all of the vivid colors and details of the trip were forever stuck in my memory, and seemed to continue to flow out through other dreams, one after another.

In the weeks that followed, my friend Carol Musser, one of my friends whom I had prayed for while spinning the prayer cylinders in the temple in Kathmandu, ended up losing her battle with her liver issue. While surrounded by her family, Carol returned her borrowed time and humbly laid it back at the feet of God on March 5, 2011. The rainy evening that she passed away, I stood looking out the window of my house and cried while remembering Carol's life and what she meant to all of us that were blessed to know her. I searched my soul to remember the words from our last conversation, and then longed to remember more than I could. I watched the rain turn to snow and eventually over the next hour it covered everything that I could see in a blanket of thick, white fluff that hung off of every branch on every bush, on every tree, turning my neighborhood into a winter wonderland. It was heavenly. I shook my head while laughing through the tears, and said out loud, "Yep, only someone like you, Muss, could get to heaven and pull strings like this." I will be forever blessed by her friendship in my life, and will never forget her ability to truly live in the moment of everything that she did. My other friends that inspired me on the trip, Judi Hamilton and Pauline Smith, continue to be the feisty versions of the woman that I hope to be in the years ahead in my life. I am blessed by every single moment that I get to spend with them. Those two ladies never take one minute for granted, and if I ever start to do that, I can guarantee you they will kick my butt and point me in the right direction. That's what good friends do when they love you.

My heart will be forever branded with the images of Amala, Bagabati and their families, and this trip made me question the amount that I am paying forward with my time and my God-given talents. Am I really doing what God wants me to be doing with the remaining years in my life, with all of the borrowed time that I have left? Those questions haunt my days, and I continue to listen for guidance and direction. I can still smell the smog in Kathmandu, and I can taste the fried cashews and chicken mo-mo. I can hear the villagers laugh and talk in a language that only they can understand, and I can feel the mud beneath my fingertips as if I was still working in those two new bamboo homes. "Kay-Kay" had experienced poverty on a different level than ever before, and there were countless times when our whole team seemed to be locked in some time warp within the simplicity of a Third World country. But my most vivid memories contain the faces of everyone that I met in Nepal, the grandeur of the Himalayan Mountains, and the sights and sounds of India. I remember smiling souls, with an inquisitive interest to understand who I was, and the willingness of so many people to share their lives with me. The face of that little Dashrath, and he and his friends greeting me with their new found American knuckle bump, will never be forgotten. And when I hug my own Mabel, I sometimes see in her eyes a bone-thin dog on the other side of the world that I hope is somehow loved by someone. I am thankful for the new friendships with my Habitat for Humanity team members, and I can't wait to get enough vacation time built up to head out on another adventure with them somewhere around the world (should they be nuts enough to ask me to tag along). None of us will ever forget the great memories of our trek through the

Himalayan Mountains, and for the opportunity to spend several days with those young men who carried our bags and became our hiking comrades and Bananagrams competitors. And wow, within three days I actually saw the Taj Mahal and a tigress in the wild, and felt flying elephant snot while getting sunburned on an elephant ride, and am *still* proud to call myself the John-and-Deb-Egli-red-headed-stepchild! Hopefully somewhere in Nepal, my once-treasured hiking boots are now being worn on another trek through the beautiful mountains that are just a spot on my floating desk globe that I gently spin with my fingertips amidst ringing phones, whizzing emails, strategic planning, and executive calendaring conundrums. Each morning, I grab my Droid, my purse and keys, put on my Parkview badge, and pat my beloved furry Flossie and Mabel good-bye. As I head out of my house, I glance up at a sign hanging at my back door that reads, "Life is good". And then I smile, because somewhere in Nepal, the knuckle bump is spreading like wildfire.

Acknowledgements

Many thanks to my family, friends, Tina and all of my Parkview co-workers, and my Habitat for Humanity cohorts for their encouragement along the journey of completing this book. This was a learning experience and life-dream-come-true for me, and I enjoyed every step of the process. I will be forever grateful to Jeff and Jodi Junkin, for their knowledge of the printing and graphic worlds, and for all of their guidance, talent, and time that they openly and willingly shared with me along the way to help a novice writer. Thanks to my "bestest-friend", Judi Hamilton, for allowing me to share her story of positive attitude and strength which we hope will inspire others who may be battling cancer. Thanks to Rick Henvey for being a great life mentor and a daily example of what it means to serve others with a compassionate spirit. Thanks to Ruben Gonzalez for his self-publishing knowledge, Catherine Wilcox for her legal guidance, Sean Westerhouse for his inspiring attitude, Jerry Youngblutt for his words of wisdom and publishing research, and my appreciation to Bill Beymer for his radiology prowess. And a very special thank-you to Steve Longo, Mike Dendinger, and Donna Bowers, for setting aside time in their own busy lives to read the book and give me their honest critique and encouraging thoughts.

Alex and Abby — I couldn't be prouder of you and your families. Ab, you were my greatest supporter to see this book through to the end. Whenever I said I wasn't sure I could do it, you were always there, pushing me along. I love you both so much.